IT'S ALL ABOUT THE BUZZ
Understanding Terrace Culture

Jason Morgan

Cover photography by Jimm Leaf

FIRST EDITION

978-1-80227-547-6: eBook
978-1-80227-548-3: paperback

Dedication

This book is dedicated to a little princess, a little girl who had the heart of a lion who never gave up and who kept fighting to the very end.

A little girl who had more fight, more life, more backbone than a hundred men put together.

A family united in support and family we mourn, for we are and forever with you.

This book is for you, Isla xxxxxx

Contents

Acknowledgements

Without the help and sheer hard work of Millie Dillane, this book would still be a concept.

Millie, you are a beautiful soul and my mate. I will love you, Mum and Dad, and the brothers till the end of time. Thank you.

A massive thank you to all the contributors who have sent pieces in for the book. They got its concept, signing up for its meaning rather than blab on about isolated incidents and slate other teams off.

Big shout out to the Everton away group: Brett (Benjamin Button), Uncle Bob, Carpy, Elliot, Chaz B, Newbury, Toffee, Billy B, Keith, Kathy, Tommy M, Joe M, Les B and all the actual inspiration for the book and massive contributors. Thanks for looking after us, and your hospitality and wit.

Thank you, Joe England, for assistance and advice.

A massive shout out to all friends, past and present, especially absent friends gone but not forgotten. You have touched all our hearts and have been a major part of our lives especially through these weird times. We salute you. We miss you. Our lives will always be missing something and hope one day we can meet again. Too many to mention but the saying is as long as you are remembered "you never die". We raise a glass to you. Alison, your star shines on. You'll never be forgotten.

Last, but not least, my family. A family who I never tire of loving, who I never regret getting up every day to provide for, who give me the strength I need to carry on. A wife who I adore. My gorgeous kids who I would give anything for and who make me proud. My nephew who I love. A mum, dad and sister who have always had my back and gave me the best start in life. And my in-laws, or out-laws (however you want to put it, lol), who I love dearly.

Footnote:

I tried to cover all walks of life and all areas. I think I might have missed a few places, teams and folk, and maybe catch up with them later. I've also left some spelling errors and grammar in as I felt it's how the punter saw it and said it. There may be some inaccuracies and sure, the PC brigade will drag me over the hot coals later, but I love a bit of slang me. I feel it represents the true masses!

Foreword

Peter Hooton – Liverpool

We all remember our first visit to a football ground. The sight of the green pitch, the distinctive smell of hot dogs and Bovril, the noise, the smell of horse manure in the middle of the road. We remember the deafening cheers, the chants and the booing, the rollercoaster of glory and the despair. The wind and the rain, the muddy pitches, the orange ball and the snow-covered pitches. As kids, we collected football cards and did swaps and pretended to be our favourite players in the park. After my granddad (who lived a stone's throw from Anfield) started kicking a ball to me, when I had barely started walking, all I ever wanted to do was play football or watch it.

My dad was a season ticket holder at Anfield from 1962 in the newly built Kemlyn Road. He also knew someone called Ray Shelley who was the son of Albert Shelley, a legend at LFC who had been a player, then the odd job man around Anfield in the 1960s. He was able to get tickets for the "obstructed view" in the main stand so my dad could take me. As soon as I heard the Kop and saw Liverpool in their all-red strip, I was hooked. As a youngster, I had no animosity towards other teams. After all, I had been collecting the likes of Bobby Moore, Peter Osgood, George Best and Martin Chivers on football cards for years.

I started going to the games without my dad in the early 70s. I went to a match against Manchester United at Anfield in the early 70s, but after sitting on a barrier near the middle of the Kop, I came off the barrier during a sway and couldn't get back to it as the crowd was so tightly packed. In those days, it was a tradition that youngsters (and women) were passed over the heads of Kopites until they reached the safety of the front. After this incident, I realised I wasn't big enough for the Kop yet. I thought I needed to go to the safety of the Anfield Road end. I went by the fence at the front as no way was I going to be seen dead with a beer crate. The first few games were fine but then, during these games, trouble started to erupt behind me, as there was no segregation. When we played Everton in March 1972, it started to get dangerous in the so-called "friendly" derby. Just before kick-off, loads of bottles started to rain down on us at the front. Heads were split open and men, women and children were being injured. I remember the Everton fullback Tommy Wright scoring an own goal at the Anny Road end in the first minute but celebrations at the front were interrupted by calls for the St John's ambulance to attend another injury.

It was at this match I thought I had to take another chance in the Kop, so I went back to the barrier I had left before. Luckily, I had grown a bit but still needed to sit on the bar. It was our bar for many years until we moved to "pot corner" in the corner of the Kop by the white wall in the 1980s. I saw many a memorable match from our bar in the Kop. The one that stands out was when we won the league at Anfield in April 1973. We had got there early, as Liverpool only needed a draw against Leicester to clinch the title, so it was bound to be a lockout. I got there about 12:30 and the crowds outside were huge but I managed to get in a couple of hours before kick-off. That wasn't unusual in those days, as the Kop would fill up and the singing would begin. Shankly's second great team lifted the trophy and went on a lap of honour followed by the great man himself. I have never witnessed scenes like it before or since. There is YouTube footage that captured his lap of honour as kids mobbed him. He walked slowly around the ground to the strains of "Shankly Shankly" to the tune of "Amazing Grace". It was never ending. It took an age for him to walk in front of the Kop as scarves were thrown towards him. It was a religious experience and he was our Messiah.

Other memorable games included a comeback against Spurs to win 3-2 when we were 2-0 down at halftime (they hadn't won at Anfield at that time since the Titanic was sunk in 1912) and the 1973 UEFA Cup final against Borussia Mönchengladbach that was rained off the first night so was ten pence to get in the following night. We got there from school early as we thought it would be a lockout with it being so cheap but everyone must've thought the same and not bothered. The gate was 41,000 and our capacity was 56,000 at the time. With Toshack back in the line-up (he had been left out the previous night for Brian Hall), the Keegan/ Toshack partnership destroyed the classy German side and Liverpool eventually lifted their first European trophy in Germany a couple of weeks later. After bitter disappointments for Bill Shankly, it was the start of a European journey that continues to this day.

I have vivid memories of my first away match against Manchester United at Old Trafford. My dad had bought two tickets from Ray Shelley who had contacts in Manchester. It was a birthday treat and I was so excited. We got to the ground and we were in the stands behind where the Liverpool fans were located. It was the season United went down and they were angry. Very angry! I just remember running battles outside, but soon we were in the safety of our seats. I could see the fighting going on. The Liverpool fans were in front of us then some of them got onto the pitch which resulted in the Stretford end running the full length of the pitch. It was reminiscent of the footage when they invaded the pitch after Denis Law's goal for City later on in the same season. It was a warzone and the match hadn't even started. As a youngster, I felt safe in the seats with my dad but what would we do if Liverpool scored? Luckily, it was a drab 0-0 affair but the hatred was an eye-opener and as we walked back to the car, I told my dad we best stay quiet. Welcome to the real world!

Even though the trip to Old Trafford had been an eye-opener, it had also whet my appetite for away games. The football specials had been banned when I started going to my first away games, so I would get on Lawrenson's or Crown coaches. But a couple of years later, they were back on. They were an experience and it's hard to describe arriving in another city getting off the special. It was unique. Warm welcomes were guaranteed in places like Birmingham, Manchester, Leeds, Middlesborough and London. The specials themselves appeared to be old rolling stock from India but they got you from A to B. But they were in a terrible state. If anyone misbehaved, they were thrown in the cage usually next to the so-called tuck shop. There were plenty of characters on the specials but one that stood out, who is no longer with us, was "Jo Jo" from Bootle who would go around the train asking for your "odds" (spare change) so he could fleece people playing cards using other people's money. He could've been a character in Catch 22. Sadly, he is no longer with us.

This book gathers the stories and memories of football fans from across the country, warts and all. It's an authentic voice of the football fan that lived through those times. In the modern day, there are so many bluffers who write books or post on football forums, that it's good the real voices of the terraces are in print for posterity. I never judge people who lived through that period, as it was a very dangerous time to be a football fan. I went because I loved football and nothing was going to stop me but I did sometimes think was it the definition of madness. Never more so than when I was kicked unconscious at White Hart Lane in 1980 after an FA Cup game. I had met some Londoners on holiday in Newquay a couple of years before, due to our mutual love of The Clash and football. They were dressed similar to us, polo shirts and Stan Smith's, but whereas most of our lot had "wedge" hairstyles, they had a variety of haircuts with only one sporting a wedge. A few supported Chelsea and some of them were Spurs and they lived in Camberwell, Peckham and Dulwich. They became good mates (and still are) and me and my mates spent many a weekend down there usually when we were playing London teams.

When we played Spurs in the Cup, I was staying with them so had to get back to their car after the match to go to a party they had arranged. If I had stayed with Liverpool fans and gone to Seven Sisters tube, I probably would've been okay, but I had to make my way back to their car, which was parked near the ground. I cut off the High Road onto a side street to double back towards the ground and their car. I had planned my route before the match but unfortunately, I bumped into a "friendly" bunch of "Donkey-jacketed" Tottenham fans. They took one look at and me and pounced. I was wearing a cagoule and sporting a pair of red Puma Argentinas. I was fast and was doing okay but then headed to an older chap who looked like "Giant Haystacks" thinking he didn't look like a hooligan. I headed towards him on the pavement but he just stuck out his enormous belly and bounced me into the privets. The last thing I remember was a voice in the crowd screaming, "Kill the Scouse c**t."

I don't know how long I was out for but I remember a Cockney voice whispering in my ear, "Out of order that. Out of order. I got them off you. I'm Millwall." I've always wondered who the good Samaritan was. An ambulance arrived and as it made its way down the High Road towards North Middlesex hospital, I could hear the mayhem outside and saw a well-known Liverpool fan being thrown through a shop window. It was one of the worst situations Liverpool had been in probably down to the sheer numbers. If 300 to 500 had been there, it would've been okay, but there were ten times that number and I think Liverpool fans had upset the Broadwater Farm "community" before the match.

I arrived at the hospital to be greeted by a cheery bunch of casualties. I seemed to be the only Liverpool fan there and one of the many Spurs fans observed, "Fackin' 'ell, Scouse, what happened to you? Run over by a bus?" Oh, how we laughed. The camaraderie in the A & E was something I would always remember, as well as the cheque I got for £1000 for criminal injuries. I lost my front teeth and had six stitches in an eye wound but thankfully my suspected "fractured skull" was ruled out after X-rays. I had concussion for a couple of weeks but apart from that, I was fine. It didn't put me off going and I never blamed Spurs fans as such. I was just in the wrong place at the wrong time. My London mates couldn't apologise enough but we all knew it was an occupational hazard in those days.

Football has been in my blood for as long as I remember and it still gets my heart racing even though it is unrecognisable from the days when I first started going. It is quite simply a drug, arguably the opium of the masses, but I just can't stop listening to fans' experiences and memories. It's the authentic voice of the voiceless and here are some of those stories. Enjoy!

Jason Morgan – West Ham

Have you ever sat on a football special on a cold winter's night heading up north or down south?

Have you ever stood in an away end, rain and sleet raining down on you, wearing only a Sergio Tacchini tracksuit and suede Adidas Gazelles soaked through to the bone?

Did you ever bunk the fares and rob some beers or nick that tracksuit?

Did you crap yourself or did you stand? Were you there for the aggro or were you a die-hard fan loyal to your club and area?

Why did you do it? Why did you keep going? Why did you go to Roker Park on that football special for six hours with ripped seats, smashed windows, stinking of piss? Why did you watch your team get stuffed then get attacked, or attack the opposing team? Why did you then get back on that train again for six hours and get home in the early hours of the morning?

There must be a reason.

I grew up in a stable home. Mum and Dad worked hard. Dad was a scaffolder. Mum kept the home then went to work when we were old enough to look after ourselves. My sister and I had love and a good upbringing.

We moved from South London to East Ham in 1975, when I was four. Who knows, if Dad had turned left instead of right, I might have been a Bushwhacker instead of a Hammer. My earliest, and probably last best memory, was West Ham winning the FA Cup in 1980. I remember the sheer jubilation and celebrations. From that day on, I wanted to be a Hammer. I would go on and off with my dad or friends up until my teens before I started going with a mob.

Those were the days when you could rock up five minutes before kick-off and pay and get in. If you were skint, you could see the last twenty minutes as they opened the gates. It was fun, carefree and easy.

There is nothing remarkable about me. I'm not a hard man, not a face. I started going properly mid to late 80s. I probably missed the boat by ten years. My reasons were born out of frustration and teenage anger. The 80s were pretty sore. There was no real identity. The days of mods and rockers, skins and punks had long since gone and we were left with the Wham factor.

Standing on the terraces, I admired the older, smarter faces and I wanted to be like them and wanted to be part of their culture. I had something to prove and that's where it started for me. I wanted to dress like them and become a face. I wanted to be as game as them. I would stand there getting abused by the away supporters in the South Bank and that's where the seed grew.

I was fronted twice when I was fourteen: outside the ground once by a Manc, then got run everywhere by Cardiff when they came to Orient. I dwelt on this for ages and my blood boiled. I met many good people and some not so good, but that's all part of it. We had some great times and some scary times. I stood alongside black and white and all walks of life in a period of civil unrest. I know what it's like to be subjected to prejudice because of class and have seen racism first hand, because I was there when it was at its most prevalent. Colour and class aside, we were all part of one culture and stood side by side. We sang, travelled, boozed, raved, fought and slept rough all in the name of one thing, and I would put my life in the hands of nearly all of them at that particular time.

Thirty years later, I still go to matches occasionally. You see, whether friends old or new, most of them I can sit with and listen to all day. We like to moan, like to reminisce about the old days.

For years, I wanted to put pen to paper and share my experiences, but I didn't want to write about the row with so-and-so, and whose firm was crap and we were the best, blah blah blah... I want to try to make people understand why I wanted to be part of the terrace culture, why it made me feel the way I did, why I felt good with a new pair of Armani jeans or tracksuit, why it felt good to belong, seeing my firm every week. Why we did what we did. Why I was buzzing all week, phoning and plotting and trying to scrape the money together. Why on Monday morning I felt so tired and dizzy, but could not wait to do it all again.

Eventually, I had enough and met a cracking girl, started a family and settled down. All things come to an end. It's not like the old days and why would I want to get in bother now? Having recently taken a trip up to Everton, we met some old foes, talked about the old days and how it was. No one gave it the big one; we all had mutual respect. What I found was different stories and different reasons why we did what we did. I want to explore and try to make people understand why we did what we did. I'm not just asking the crews, but die-hard supporters too. I don't want to know about the day they rumbled this team and that team. I want to know why they got involved and how it made them feel and what they think of the present.

If you can imagine being frightened but excited at the same time, then you might appreciate what I'm on about. One of our mates, a very game chap called Tony W, was telling us about going up to Everton in the 80s and how naughty it was, how electric and tense the atmosphere was; how sheer hatred and pride for their city made it a formidable place to go. Getting out of there in one piece and having been there to front it out made for a madly intense and exciting experience.

I was very naïve back in the day. I thought a trip up north or over to bandit country would be a day out with a bit of aggro, but in no short time, I was very wrong. My eyes were open to the pure hatred the other teams had for us.

I remember two savage outings to Millwall. I kid you not, it was like Beirut. To this day, it's a blur. The whole time all I could do was survive the day. Coming back, I felt elation and bravado but inside, I was just glad we made it back. Going up to Liverpool in the mid-80s was the same. We got pelted on the coach from the station to the ground. The houses were derelict and there was lots of wasteland where young scallies would pop up like meerkats and launch bottles at us. Again, I was naïve to what had been going on in Liverpool in the early 80s where there had been civil unrest, pure hatred of authority and outside influence or outsiders end of. The scallies were one of the forerunners on the fashion front and were one of the first jibbers and mass raiders of shops, home and abroad, where they would procure the latest fashionable items at said discounted rates.

The further north you got, such as Newcastle, Middlesbrough, Sunderland, it was like a different planet. They would froth at the mouth and run through a brick wall to get at you. They hated southerners and our flashy nature just added fuel to the flames. The miners' strikes were just finishing and southern coppers were getting huge overtime to go up north to crack skulls. They weren't shy at rubbing it in, so the hatred for us was further intensified. Going right up north, the especially poxy journey, and usually on a cold wet night made for a hellish experience. The firms from the Midlands, coming off the back of the Handsworth riots of 1981, was another hotbed of hatred. The Midlands are massive and contain numerous naughty firms, made up of people of varying races. People talk about racism and make assumptions, but most firms had lots of black and white blokes, who were overprotective of their image and territory, and weren't gonna lay down or let you get away lightly when going up there. The Yorkshire lads came from big industrial communities, like Sheffield and Leeds. They grew up in massive social circles where they worked hard and drank hard and were proud of their towns. They weren't having anybody larging it around their manor, and those towns and cities were not a good place to wander onto an estate or get lost.

The West Country mobs, ranging from Portsmouth, Southampton and Plymouth, were naval towns historically where sailors would drink and fight and the place was always naughty to go to. All these places historically, ranging from West Ham/East London where we had the Thames Iron Works, the docks at Millwall, the industrial towns of Sheffield, the mining towns up north and the docks of Liverpool, were hard working, playing pits of vice and violence. We were the second-generation post-war and watched and listened to our grandads, dads and uncles tell their tales of bravado and their dislike for other areas of the country. We came from civil unrest, mass unemployment and poor political motivation. We had nothing to look forward to but every Saturday, we were up and down the country and we would vent our anger and frustrations by abusing, or wanting to kick seven bells out of, the opposition. Sorry, it sounds a bit vulgar, a bit crass, but coming from that period of time, it was all we had.

Thinking further afield and whilst writing this piece, I thought long and hard about many other things that influenced me during this period and throughout my life. I mean, what other things kept me going through these uncertain times? Well, it was always good to watch a good film, maybe something that struck a chord with my life. I remember watching *Quadrophenia* by the Who 'till the tape wore out. I remember to this day most of the scenes and the lines. I remember how the main character Jimmy would build up his dull week at work looking forward to the weekend: going out with his mates, popping pills and causing mayhem. He would wake up Monday morning feeling rough and miserable, having to force himself back into the rat race until the next weekend where he came to life again. Then, eventually breaking down, giving it all up and going on a one-man mission to self-destruction. I saw a lot of myself in Jimmy. I saw a lot of mates based around central characters and on reflection, could have taken Jimmy's path and ended up far worse off in life.

I guess the escapism of fantasy and relating to these characters helped me through these uncertain times thinking, *If someone has taken time to write about this character then they have been this character and I'm not the only one going through this melancholy.* Looking from the outside in, I realised that ultimately when the party's over, I'm afraid life really has to go on and you have to accumulate the beer vouchers and be part of the system.

What else? Well, the most obvious was the music scene. It went hand in hand with the casual scene and life in general. A thousand times I went to bed, earphones in hand, playing music until I crashed out. Those were the days when it was a record player which would automatically restart the record and would be on repeat throughout the night, so I would wake up in the morning, ears ringing, and have an entire album go through my head all day.

Before football, I was mainly training and competing at judo, hanging out with mates, etc. but always liked my music. We used to have dedicated record shops but remember Woolworths on East Ham high street and buying my first record. I know it was Tenpole Tudor either "Swords of a Thousand Men" or "Throwing My Baby Out With the Bath Water". This was around 1980, and I would buy one per week with whatever pocket money I could get or earn. Sadly, none were saved. They're all gone now.

Growing up in the 80s was strange. Although, looking back, there was some great music. It was a bit camp, a bit Wham factor and trying to be cool or trying to be a chap didn't sit right. As I explained earlier, there wasn't a movement such as mods and rockers, and punk and skinheads were dying out. We were either going to wear our "Choose Life" T-shirts, or after watching Wimbledon took the Fila/Bjorn Borg approach which sort of defined the casual movement.

Don't get me wrong, I wasn't anti-Wham. I quite like them, but my macho side needed something else. So, around 1984, aged thirteen, I would try to aspire slowly to the look. I went to a few away games still looking like a kid and wasn't taken seriously, but still had a good buzz and looked up to the chaps.

For a few years, this game played out and by the time I was big enough, circa 1989, the casual scene was dying out and the rave scene was coming in full force. Even to this day, head-fuck or what, I still couldn't get my head 'round trying to smash an opposing team up Saturday morning only to be cuddling the life out of them Saturday night down Echo's at Bow. I remember saying to Andy S one night that these guys were trying to stab me up earlier now we are all in love. Oh, the power of ecstasy and rave music...

The fashion of this era was shocking. We tried to wear something that looked smart during the day but would fit in at night and so came the rave/casual look my end, which made me look like one of the flower pot men. I had a mullet-come-perm, wore kickers and wallabies, and goodness knows why, dungarees. I looked a right c**t!

At this time, there were some of the most memorable bands and concerts and I list below my top five, in order of best nights out, ever:

- Happy Mondays, Wembley '89 (sorry, Keith)
- The Farm at the Astoria around the same time
- Madness, Finsbury Park (Sid B might remember date)
- Bad Manners, Huntingdon Beach, California 1990
- And last, but not least, yes, I am going to get absolute pelters for this. And yes, he's a total wrong'un, but one of the Gary Glitter concerts of the time (no more needs to be said)
- Honourable mention: Much later was the Prince's Trust gig by The Who at the Royal Albert Hall with Boydy my life-long mate and brother (best gig ever)

Happy Mondays Wembley '89 was a mental night out with Dev, Jon B, Adam S. Loads of West Ham there. Mancs kicking off in the lower tiers, but what a night.

The Farm at the Astoria with the usual suspects was up there with the best nights out ever. They put on one of the best live performances along with me and Johnny B being off our tits. Then it started snowing internally. I freaked out and starting cuddling Johnny B thinking I was freezing and John, jaw swinging about like a tumble dryer, said not to worry, he would keep me warm, and cuddled me to death for the rest of the poxy night. That's good old uncle John for you (lol).

Madness at Finsbury Park. An all-dayer again. Slightly off our tits, but not off our tits, with Sid B, I think Vinny, maybe Jimmy B, Adam, Dev and Bott again. Ian Dury and the Blockheads stole the show. Madness were the nuts. So many funny things happened that day, I was so mellow and happy. It was music and good mayhem; no one got hurt. That was really one of the last bastions of live music and mayhem of that era and one I'll never forget.

Bad Manners at Huntington Beach, California in 1990. Me and Darren W borrowed Darren's brother's RV and stayed on the beach. We had a Union Jack sticker in the window. Sometime in the evening, there was a knock at the door and both shitting ourselves as to who would answer (scared of getting jacked), I think we both answered the door to find Dougie Trindle, aka Buster Blood Vessel, standing there. We invited him and the band in for a beer and the next night were on the guest list at the Brown Bear club. What a night. We partied after on their tour bus, got to meet the band and the "Skatelites", who backed them and had the best time ever. Dougie is all right for a Gooner!

Won't bang on about number five. This was before we knew he was a wrong'un, but you can't erase the past and deny that him and his band could put on a show.

Well, that was the end of the 80s and early 90s. Looking back, I preferred the 80s as the 90s was a darker era. The cocaine revolution took over, and to this day, I still cannot see the attraction but it caught up with a lot of people. I saw huge changes in myself and the people around me. The fun seemed to go out of life. There was nothing new for me, nothing original, nothing that hadn't been done. It was time for Jimmy to realise what it was all about. I met my future wife and settled down.

Prior to meeting Jen, I could be out of control and was fighting these demons. There were several people who took time out to stick with me and who I will never forget. Some are not with us: Johnny P, Brad T, Ergal, Uncle Norm and Colin M. They all took me under their wing and steered me in the right direction.

The elder members of the Hammers football team did the same, the Dillane family, Karen and George B, Billy Shipman, Old Man Pat K, Gary S, Steve B, Uncle Azza and many others put a hand on my shoulder and said, "You come from a good family. You are not a bad kid. Stop playing up. Think for a minute. Stop trying to prove yourself. The world doesn't hate you." Then I grew up a bit.

I'd like to give thanks to my life-long pals (they know who they are, the proper ones), Vinny P, Lee D and Sid B, Dev and Boydy, Craig D, Micky M and the guys at The Tokei and Metro, Mum, Dad, Suzanne, Jen's lot and anyone who started me on this journey and tried to help me stay on the path.

I look back and have cold shivers at some of the things we did or had done to us, and how many times it could have gone horribly wrong. I'm glad it never went too far. I wish I could only say that for some of the other poor folk who got caught up and paid the price either way, but such is life. I would change some of it though. I know people say they wouldn't, but I would. I think drugs are a waste of time. I'm not going to preach or look down on anyone for using them, but they just didn't agree with me. It was part of the culture of the time, but I just didn't get on with them.

I enjoyed the banter, and forming friendships and alliances. I liked the music of the era and how easy and accessible things were back then, such as just rocking up and paying to get in somewhere. I still look back and am in awe of the fashion of the time and still love the look of the chaps of the day. I also like how basic the technology of the time was. I used to get my messages from my mum when I got in or even at the Hammers pub. Mobile phones can be very handy but I see them as intrusive and evasive and I am a Big Brother theorist.

On the subject of racism, I am afraid that it gets up my nose. I grew up in a very multicultural environment. I have many close friends from a whole range of backgrounds and cultures and most of them I would trust with my life. I do not support any form of hate crime or persecution. I have no time for politicians. I think they are all liars who don't give two hoots about us. I have lived through a time of racial hatred and been subjected to class abuse. I lived in a period where, black or white, you were hated by the police and higher classes and looked down on; a time where there was cause for complaint. We were not angels. We were framed half the time, but got away with more than we got stitched up for. I have no complaints. I believe that most of the people that are trying to cause and stir up trouble on the subject of racial hatred in today's society are just jumping on the bandwagon. There are other outside influences and agencies that are using this as an excuse to cause trouble in the name of their own causes.

I am glad I was born in an era where I saw first-hand these abuses and how races and lower classes dealt with this and grew above the hatred. I feel very sorry for the folk who genuinely suffer any form of abuse but have no time for snowflakes who pretend. Speak to the ones who were there and they will tell you how it is.

Now I've had my rant, have a read and see what you think.

Ricky W – Cardiff

I am a man of fifty-two summers and grew up in a decent working-class area of Cardiff known as Splott.

I had a healthy and busy childhood that indicated in no way the path I took as a teenager. Disruptive, argumentative and cheeky, my elders would call it. Adventurous is what I called it.

Late 70s and early 80s in Splott, you were either a mod, punk, skin, rude boy or into Status Quo and Motorhead. I chose the mod route having a big thing about The Jam.

With this, came risks and challenges. Challenges that would steer me towards gang fights and general unruly behaviour.

The music was a big part of my growing up. The first band 1 saw live were Bad Manners. Spent most of the afternoon with them as my mum was a cook in Cardiff students' union canteen and worked the bar in the events hall in the establishment. I had the freedom of the place that day, watched the sound check, watched the band eat and finally watched them play to a half-full concert hall.

So, the path I took was an eventful one because whatever cult you chose, you would clash with those you didn't choose. Mods had "enemies": punks, skins and the new lot, trendies, who were basically the younger element of Cardiff City football firm. Now, I was also a massive football fan and Cardiff were my hometown team. My uncle took me and my cousin to the home games and the splendid surroundings of Ninian Park would stay with me forever. God, I miss that place.

I was not fully aware of football violence at this time but I knew that the trendies would offer an opposition for us young mods as did the skins. Many a Saturday afternoon was spent playing cat and mouse around Cardiff city centre. It was always full-on conflict with full-on contact. Not the usual school scrap which was mostly one on one. This was different. This was group brawling. I fucking loved it. I was hooked.

As a small group of mods, we mastered the art of sticking together and not running. The tear ups were spontaneous with windmills and shit 'off balance kicks but they seemed to work for a while. Then with pubic hair came teaching tools in the form of films and videos. *McVicar* and *Scum* were watched over and over. The buzz of the violence you were viewing was like a schooling, watching your first head (but on the telly), then spending the next few nights re-enacting and practising it in the mirror and against the door.

I remember the first man fight I saw. We lived in a terraced house fifty metres from the Splott Conservative Club and a few drunken brawls had my full attention.

Bingo and an idea. Our little group would seek new opposition and pick fights with the drunks leaving the local clubs and pubs. Our youth and nimbleness gave us good odds and results, but you never forget the first real hard punch you receive. Well, I fucking didn't. I can still smell the offending fist. I had been punched and kicked by my age group for years. In a boxing ring, in the playground, in town. It was just part of growing up. But to feel the force of a man you just kicked in the knee... well, that's different. Nevertheless, I had this sick liking of the adrenaline rush, heart pounding and hyperventilating of a ruck and getting your hands dirty. I was hooked.

With my attendance at football home games, I began to recognise the groups. Those who were my age on the edges, then those a few years older who seemed very

3

active and were now called the "Soul Crew". This name has stuck to this day and was created by one of these older lads on a return train journey from a Wokingham FA Cup game in the autumn of 1982.

Now the ironic thing is the trendies and skins, who were my opponents in the very early mod days, turned into the very people I would spend the next forty years with. People who I have spent all my Saturdays with, sat in a pub miles from home, in a town or city you have never been to before. These people you call mates whose friendship and loyalty extends beyond the football. We grew from little groups from across the city and surrounding valleys into a unit.

You find yourself gelling with likeminded gentlemen. With similar interests, similar morals, full of dignity and pride. But most of all, the invisible filtration system that was in place. People come and go and the wrong'uns are soon moved on and if you didn't belong then you knew it. Nothing wrong with that. I am a fond believer in surrounding yourself with likeminded folk who don't take. They give and rely on you as much as you rely on them. This was the Saturday family and stretched much further than just a few beers and a twenty-man brawl. Be it at the football, holidays, Europe, club, bar, railway station or weddings, funerals, christenings, engagement parties and most of life's celebrations, we were together.

The word loyalty is used far too frequently, but we knew its meaning and just how important it was. I used to preach my saying, "the only key that will unlock the padlock of power is the key of loyalty." Most would laugh, but history has proven this to be true.

We looked out for each other and if you stepped out of line, you were quickly upheld and brought back down. If you didn't have something or could not do something, someone in the Saturday family would.

Lots call these groups firms or crews and I get that but we were simply likeminded gents who respected right from wrong, respected each other and respected that there were groups like us all over the country. We were all Cardiff fans and we all liked a bit of knuckle, didn't mind hurting these other groups, but never wanted to maim them either.

Before I touch on the violence and buzz from it, I think the culture that is still encapsulating these groups needs to take stage.

Clothes, trainers... now we are talking.

This was a culture that made labels massive. A culture with a forever changing uniform. A uniform that was great to wear first and even better when every c**t copied you. I get the ever-changing new brand but for me it's the clobber you always liked: the smarter casual pristine look. Guess that's the mod in me. Was never fussed on the tennis look. Some tracksuits were like a Brighton beach deck chair. I did like the harlequin blouson leather and suede jackets. The long paisley shirts with long round backs untucked. Loved Farah and we made the effort of cutting the labels off, splitting the seams up an inch and plonking the label at the top of this cut. Wasn't fussed on the broaches worn with the paisley shirts but appreciated the top button done up. Patrick cagoules, Lois cords, boat shoes. They ticked the boxes. Lacoste was always smart and timeless but fucking expensive (especially when your apprentice wages were not great). I still wear some of the old BASI labels I still have and wear silver croc and massive V. The modern Lacoste just ain't as good quality. Denvenlay sub out the manufacture. Some of the stuff made in the US just did not last as long.

Early Giorgio Armani collection gear with the stitched-on gold eagle were class. Still own a few. Emporio Armani jumpers, sweatshirts with the huge crest and red globe were great quality. I sold all mine when my kids were born because they were too tight and fetching good money on the bay. Sold most of it for more than I paid for it.

Paul&Shark from the early and mid-90s was classic: crew neck and V-neck jumpers with elbow patches and buttons on the shoulder, proper yachting gear. Still got it all. Gave a huge bag full to my eldest lad who asked if I had ever heard of it. His face was a fucking picture. Spent two days on the phone tilling his peers and clan.

Same as early Stone Island. Kept it all. Most of the jackets are fucked, peeling everywhere, a few battle scars, tears and splits. But kept the lot and gave them to my lad as it's a label that's been reborn. Too much for me though as some of the pieces were unique and you never saw another. Not like today where there is five in all sizes on the rail, even in the official SI stores.

As for the knuckle, we had numbers, but that was more of a hindrance rather than an asset. Some of the numbers we pulled out for some games were unreal. However, the better dancing was had when we kept it to a baker's dozen and moved away from the masses. The group would swell from time to time, but it was a decent group of chaps who knew each other inside out. Trust, loyalty experience and a mentalist element kept us together. If you fucked up, you were told. If you didn't perform, you never lived it down.

We had success and failure. Those who say they never get backed off or turned over must be a special kind of force. We got done and admitted it. We had good results and still talk about them. The upper hand we achieved on occasions was only counted as we stuck together and had a bit of quality. But more was due to the fear factor. Or was it fearless factor? Some proper mad c**ts in the group never failed to amaze me on just how potty they were. Been picked up off the floor many a time, had broken bones, and scars all over my bonce and face. Been bottled, hit with all sorts, even had a plant pot smashed over my head. But you have to be in it to win it.

Never been a fan of weapons and was always of the opinion that you want to hurt the opposition and not maim them. Never got the knife thing or anyone who carried one, just not our thing.

Gas was trendy in the early 90s and worked to good effect. Been on the receiving end of that a few times and you really are out of the action for forty-five minutes when you take it full on. This is a weapon that has mass effect and will stop a decent sized mob if used properly. The off shore opposition are fond of it and use it in the strangest of places. Standard Liège used it on us in a café in '93. Wiped everyone in the place. There were uneaten croissants and pastries on every table. Even the waitress got wiped out.

The same lot (Belgians) came to us mid-80s for an international qualifier. They were a strange lot. Some of them dressed like The Fonz. We took it to them all day but the best result was when the sun went down. They were holed up in a bar on a busy road in the city centre. We went for it and they obliged. I saw and felt something new that night. They spread into the street and looked like a scene from *West Side Story*. All in leather jackets and dancing. Our front line ran straight into them. BOSH! My nose was hanging off (again). Without getting close enough to twat one of them, I was out of the action. They had taken their belts off with huge buckles. An effective weapon if they connected to your boat race. I can vouch for that. Think I got hit by a Harley Davidson buckle.

I left the scene in a mess and A & E beckoned. In them days, I had a membership to the place. While I was swerving the chaos in the street, I did glance at the melee. There were three of our younger lot hanging onto this beast who was swinging them around like a fairground carousel.

This beast we encountered earlier. I had given him my best shot from the side, but the c**t didn't move.

9

Fuck. But he took a clout from behind and it gave me a chance to move onto the next victim. The beast looked like a Hell's Angel with a leather waistcoat.

After my failure to make an impression on both encounters, I left the dressing room of A & E having stitches added to my ever-changing nose profile. And there he was laid out and spilling all over the trolley in the corridor. He looked fucked and his eyes were closed. Bingo! I wasn't gonna miss this opportunity. As I passed him, I gave him a nice elbow to his nose. It cracked and he moved this time with a very loud yelp, but I was off.

The hospital corridor had a few patients all gasping with shock. I shouted out, "That's what you get when you hit old ladies, ya fat twat," as I made my exit. Nothing ever came of it. There were no cameras in A & E in them days and my leaving comment may have helped me with the witnesses.

Good battles off shore were a regular for us. Cardiff was quite often in the Cup Winners' comp after winning the Welsh Cup. Belgium, Germany, Denmark... just to name a few where we got our hands dirty.

I lost interest in watching Wales away for years when my kids were born. I got the bug back now after recent success and the Euros were a blast. Not so much for violence but for the same old faces. Just different places and the factor of being off shore with your now aging group.

I still look at my old yearly passports and my nose is a different shape in each one. Guess that tells a story.

I could go on and on about "we did this, we did that" but it's all been said and done before. Some exaggerate and others lie. The facts are there and if you really have to embellish the event then you probably weren't there. It amazes me how much detail people put into describing a scrap. How they can remember it all baffles me. Once the starter pistol goes, I am off. Hyperventilating, adrenaline pumping, urging for the first contact. I know what's in front of me, got a good idea of what's behind me and I know who is standing next to me. This never really changed. I couldn't tell you what fucking top he was wearing or what trainers he had on. The violence takes over here, nothing else matters. Let's go, looking for the first shoulder drop of off-balance stance just to get the upper hand. Then spending the next fifteen minutes catching your breath back and checking for injuries. Then the euphoria of the dance and worry if it had been captured on film. The inevitable knock on the door and yet another conviction.

11

This is where it ends. Cameras killed it off. Over-passionate policing and a mission for the football OB to capture the ring leaders and the names that matter.

Technology and stitch ups take their toll. It's over. Fact.

Today's lads never had like we did. Far more to lose: minimum three-year ban, FBO, passport confiscation. Not a £30 fine and a year's ban that you never adhered to.

We never had a deterrent. We never had CCTV footage of our get togethers. We never had a group of mobile phones capturing every move. Fuck that. Unless I can guarantee total zero consequences, I am not getting my hands dirty anymore.

Too many scars, too many convictions. Jail and fines do work. I am out.

But it's a great trade-off for the buzz, the memories, the chaps and the opposition you have met over the years.

Great lads from WHU, Hull, Wigan, Wall, Plymouth... Lads just like yourself, only different accents.

We still get the odd event and what we call "rack n roll" violence. Lots of our lot are into music and gigs. You quite often get a group of not-so-friendly fans in the crowd. Be it at home, Bristol or London. It's always a good platform to perform and as it's not "football", the consequences on the whole are minimal.

We loved to leave before halftime. A baker's dozen. It worked well as we always found the dancefloor came unstuck a few times but that's the nature of the beast. Feed the habit, so to speak.

These days the violence is a fond memory. Still watch the same team, still travel all over the country, still wear the same clothes and still drink with the same faces.

The Saturday family. Mates forever.

I miss the smell of the old stadiums. I miss the smell of the old football trains. I miss the motorway service station encounters.

I miss the £2.50 ground entrance fees.

I miss getting off the train knowing it was there waiting for you if you wanted it.

I miss the pubs closing at 3 p.m. as you know you had to get to the ground.

I miss the hot OXO that kept your hands warm on cold November nights.

I still have all these memories and I still share them with the gentlemen I created them with.

I write this during the second lockdown, where every game I have watched via the TV and media steams, across the Prem, Champ, League 1, League 2. Or how I preferred it, Division 1-2-3-4.

Boring. My two boys' park football games gave me more pleasure.

Point to not football is a fans' thing.

Anyway, my point is I miss the lads, the banter, the clothes the beer, the gear, the handshakes, the hugs and the smiles. The stories of old, the talk of other firms, the "I'll be home before MOTD" comment as you leave ya missus on the front door followed by her reply, "no fighting". It wasn't just about the knuckle. It was about the congeniality we shared on a Saturday.

I miss the Saturday family.

Take my boys. These days, football is so different now. But we had it when it was a real feature of your upbringing and where Saturdays were Saturdays, and you checked the pools coupon and read the football echo. The only time you used a phone was in the custody suite using your "one phone call" option.

No one can take that away ever. It was ours.

Steven "Chas" B – West Ham

The first time I saw West Ham was in 1973 with Brian Yeo's testimonial at the Priestfield Stadium in Gillingham. It was local to me and I got to see my hero: Bobby Moore. My uncle took me as my dad was working nights. The first time I went to Upton Park was '77: a 1-0 loss to Aston Villa. I fell in love with the place, getting off the tube and walking along Green Street, the buzz, and an early sense of something special.

I came from a working-class family. Both my mum and dad, and later me, worked at a car factory. I played football most Saturdays and Sundays to a fairly decent level, so I didn't start going to watch matches regularly until the early 80s. Saturdays used to be a release. We were in one of the worst recessions the country had seen. It provided a sort of belonging and coming together with likeminded mates. I come from Rainham in Kent which still has a large West Ham following. I started to go with a few mates I had grown up with and it was all a bit of a laugh. We used to run the gauntlet on the train. It used to be full of Chelsea and Arsenal fans. Not so many Tottenham fans back in the day.

The Valentine's Day Massacre at Chelsea in '81 stands out as a good day. I was sixteen. A mad, mad day. I wasn't fazed by it but found the whole experience exciting on another level. Getting nicked on the first game of the season after being promoted against Brighton wasn't one of my best moves. Some of my pals dropped out in the early 80s but I had got the bug and still have to some extent. I soon got to know the regular crowd that went away and would arrange to meet them. That's if my old man wrote the message down properly after answering the old school house phone.

With away games, it was more word of mouth: "We are meeting at Euston, Saturday, Mancs away. Be at the station, don't be late." I was now working, and trust me, your wages went a long way back then. You could easily get to an away game on twenty-five to thirty pounds and still bring change home. We didn't have mobiles to ask your mates to hang on while your train up from Kent was being delayed. I met some good lads in the early days that took me under their wing. I would count down the days at work from the Monday morning in anticipation of an away game on the Saturday. It's what I lived for.

My wages went on football, fashion and beer. I have always loved my clobber and when the casual scene came along, that for me was one of the best eras for clothes. I used to shop in Stuart's on Wardour Street and Swanks was around the corner. I used Supreme Fashions down Carnaby Street for Pringle. Also, Olympus Sports on Oxford Street for trainers. The best for freebies was Lilywhites at Piccadilly Circus and Sharpe Sports in Kensington.

I met my missus in '86 and we are still going strong. She has always got me when it comes to football. Throughout the mid-80s until the early 2000s, I hardly missed a Saturday home game, even mugging off my stepbrother's wedding to go to Liverpool. I was forever bunking off work to go to night games, home and away. It was a way of life, just the natural thing to do. I got into plenty of scrapes.

One of the worst (although a funny, eventful evening) was getting nicked at Manchester City away at Maine Road in November '84 for a Milk Cup game. My mum was at home dying of cancer. When I came home the next day with my face f**ked up after getting a good shoeing off the Old Bill, my old man went bananas.

Away games provided a proper buzz and it was cheap to travel. Persil railcards, later replaced by the Young Person's railcard, were a lifesaver. On the train or coach, the camaraderie, piss-taking and banter were all part and parcel of the day. The adrenaline would kick in as you arrived at the station. If you got nicked on the day, it was just bad luck, an occupational hazard, done and dusted on the day. There was no CCTV, no getting your door hoofed in six months later and certainly no being put up on social media fifteen minutes after the ref blows for full time. Getting back from a mid-week away game and having to hang around Euston, St Pancras and King's Cross etc. all night, waiting for the first Victoria train out back to Kent was murder. It was easier in the days when you could blag the paper train home, pull the emergency cord to pre-warn the driver to let you off at your stop and you'd jump off covered in newspaper print.

I have met mates for life at football. I've been to their milestones ranging from twenty-first to fiftieth birthdays, weddings and sadly funerals. The lot. I wouldn't change anything for the world, in fact I'd go back and do it all again in a heartbeat.

Peter F – Manchester City

26.09.1979 Man City versus Sunderland. Result: 1-1

My first experiences of both football and casual culture occurred at roughly the same time. My first proper game was a night match at Maine Road. I went with my best mate at the time called Psycho, not because he was one, but merely due to his surname being Sykes. We were both twelve years old, and amazed at being allowed to go alone. I don't remember much about the game as I was in total awe of the atmosphere, the smells of the burger vans frying onions, the noise and movement of the crowd, getting crushed against the rails when we scored, and the crowd of the Kippax surging forwards in celebration. The most impressive thing was seeing a copper catch a thrown firework in his gloved hand that had been launched towards the segregation section. I was hooked over the years.

Travelling around the country in the backs of rental vans, on Donald Frances' mainline coaches, or my preferred method: good old British rail normal services, avoiding police escorts and generally causing mayhem freely.

At around the same time, my next-door neighbour took me to his mate's house. He was called Huggie and was a rich kid from Persia. He was wearing a Lacoste polo shirt and it was the first time that I'd ever seen anything like it. They explained to my green ears that all the top boys were wearing it and other luxury sports brands. Over the coming months of attending more matches, I observed, listened and learnt. Sometime towards the end of the school year, we went on a five-day trip to North Wales. The intention being to learn about geography or something of the sort. Long story short, it was at an outdoor centre and on the last day, I managed to steal a white Fred Perry polo shirt from the changing room that belonged to one of the Scousers that were in residence at the time. Hence began my lifelong love of all things *casual,* and in particular René Lacoste's crocodile.

We all have a thousand tales to tell, all growing up at roughly the same time. We only scratch the surface and the evolution of both the game and the culture that still goes hand in glove.

I think the thing for us all was the sense of belonging and being part of something, going to other cities and taking the piss, having a laugh and creating memories and bonds.

Dave F – Everton

I am a football fan. I was born into a family of football fans. My dad played to a decent standard. His father managed local and regional football. My maternal grandmother would later go on to be a season ticket holder at my club which she maintained until she could no longer climb the Bullen's Road stairs. My uncle Norman still has the seat to this day.

One of my first memories is waking up in my bedroom and wondering who the blond fella holding the Cup in the picture on my wall was, and why did he scribble on my photo? I later learnt that it was Alex Young. I remember so clearly queuing up with my mother for my dad's Cup final ticket in 1966 before my third birthday. Shortly afterwards, I was introduced to Alan Ball and my search for a hero in life came to an end. My grandparents lived within walking distance of Goodison Park and my granddad would take me to the games. From that point onwards, it was all over for me. Everything would always be about Everton FC.

My earliest match day role models were my dad's mates. They remain amongst the funniest men I have ever met. Hard working, hard swearing, drinking and smoking and they absolutely loved the Toffees. I just wanted to be them. I still do. These were big men physically, but one of them had a green Mini in which we would all bail into to drive to the game. I have been to a lot of football games in my life all over the place and heard some funny things, but these fellas were genuinely hilarious, even though I wasn't really supposed to be listening. The words they used and how they said them had me in bits. As a seven, eight, nine-year-old I was thinking to myself, *This is it. This is what I want. Where do I sign?*

I continued to go with my dad and his mates until senior school – away games as well as home. Then, like everybody else, I began to go with my mates and the elder lads. I embraced the whole lifestyle: football, clothes, music, politics and experience. Like a long-lost lover, she was the one. I was at senior school in the mid to late 70s, a period when our neighbours were ripping it up both domestically and in European competition. Yet while there were a few go-the-game R*ds, the overwhelming majority were match-attending Toffees. Home and away. I still see some of the same lads doing the same thing, only with their own children and grandchildren in tow these days.

We would often walk to school, to save bus fares, and have no dinner in order to get money to travel away. And bunk school to go to Goodison to buy tickets. Good times. In 1976-77, my club enjoyed Cup runs. We ended up getting to the League Cup final – added to at that point, an unprecedented two replays only to lose in extra time. And the FA Cup semi-final whereupon we were blatantly robbed by Clive Thomas prior to being slammed in the replay by our neighbours. I was present at them all, yet within this ultimate despair my abiding memories of that time are of Toffees bouncing. Grounds like Sunderland, Middlesbrough, Leeds United, West Ham, Chelsea, Sheffield Wednesday, the Manchester clubs and of course our neighbours, amongst many others, are clear recollections whilst most of those grounds have either changed beyond all recognition or have disappeared altogether.

Straight from school at fifteen years old, I went on my initial European jaunt via a Transalpino trip to Antwerp to watch Everton. It would open my mind to both continental culture and travel, although a more immediate impact was made by sitting in bars drinking late into the night with the older lads. Many of my contemporaries on that trip remain my friends and match attending blues to this day. Terrace culture, as it would begin to be termed, was my life and that of my friends. Ticking off the grounds, generally with various kick-offs, the clobber, the camaraderie, the specials, the ordinary, hitch-hiking. I loved it all.

Another aspect of life of the period was music. Huge. Listening to John Peel in my early teens was as much a part of my life as football. Fortunately, we had a reputable venue in town: Eric's. At Eric's, all up-and-coming bands would play and where the management both recognised and facilitated the youth audience by initiating matinee (non-alcoholic) performances. My first gig was one such matinee. The Clash at Eric's, July 1978. I was fourteen years old. I think it cost £3. I am very proud of that fact. I would go on to be a member at the club for the next few years and would see many bands and artists. The Specials, Madness, SLF, Undertones, The Buzzcocks, The Damned, Joy Division to name a few. The DJ would play punk, reggae, ska and everything in between.

The timings, Saturday teatime, ensured that home games could be arranged to end before it was off to a gig. These days, gigs, along with football, would provide me with as many life lessons as the whole of my schooling and I wish I could do it all over again. Ironically, my best mate today is a guitarist in The Farm and sits next to me at Goodison. He was often in the same room watching the same bands all those years ago and we didn't know each other. It was then and remains a small world at times.

In any review of these times, it would be remiss of me not to mention the fact that the early 1980s also saw the introduction of drugs, specifically heroin, into my area. As with most things of the time, football lads would generally be first around it and in certain cases, including my own, that is what happened. Let me clarify that this was the first time the nation had been introduced to street heroin. An epidemic ensued. There were no past experiences to learn from. No, just say no. Many I know did not come out the other side.

Politics had also been an incidental part of my life, as long as football had been, given my father was a shop steward and was always talking (some say moaning) about it. Plus, I was his eldest child and only son. I could recite that stuff like my times tables. In the same week I left school, Thatcher became prime minister and immediately targeted my region. This is not a retrospective party political broadcast, and I wish to stress that aspect but the Tories were a prominent part of life on Merseyside in the 1980s, simply upon the basis of the cabinet actively proposing and then planning the "managed decline" of the city of Liverpool and its environs. This is a documented fact and the official evidence is available to view on the internet.

The upshot for our lives and society was that our fathers lost, or were soon to lose, their jobs and very, very few of my mates were employed. Many of us would have to leave the area for work. Some never returned. Many lads continued the football on a commuter, more often a hitch-hiking, basis. I was to become one of these whilst simultaneously "squatting" on the Old Kent Road during the latter half of the decade.

Clothes, or colloquially "clobber", have been another constant in my life. I have a picture from a school charity day in May 1979 where, with approximately thirty people in the image, including a future chairman of the Football Association, I am the only person wearing Adidas (and a ski coat). My point being that it was always thus. Labels I wore then were Adidas, Lois, Pringle, Fila, Tacchini, Best Company, Lacoste. You could recognise football lads on a crowded street simply by what they wore and how they wore it. Indeed, it seems everybody these days dresses like we did as kids, including nans going to Asda. It has become ubiquitous, universal and cultural. Whereas our fathers wore smart suits in their twenties and thirties, they looked like their dads a little bit too much. Our lot would change all that. And in my opinion, it shall be the thing my generation will be ultimately remembered for.

The main memory I take from the 1970s and 80s is of course football, specifically the mid-1980s. As an Evertonian, it is the law. Having meandered through the previous decade, plus in the wake of Alan Ball's departure, salvation would ultimately be provided by his old mates and fellow members of the Holy Trinity: Howard Kendall and Colin Harvey. Like a holiday romance (lasting nearly four years), success would blaze into our lives like the sun giving us players such as Southall, Reid, Sheedy, Steven, Stevens et al. before a huge Heysel-shaped asteroid would suddenly and wholly unexpectedly smash into us and destroy all that was good and true in the world.

Our return to prominence in the English game alongside Liverpool, whom in fairness had cleaned-up domestically and in Europe for years, became our whole region's raison d'etre of the period. It was a totem. A rallying point. Case in point, Derek Hatton's famous, "Last one out, turn the lights off" quote prior to the 1984 League Cup final. It was the only thing we had to shout about and tied directly back to the anti-T*ry feeling noted earlier. The games themselves will live with me forever. Indeed, I have recently been involved in making a film of our experiences, *Everton Howard's Way Not*, the BBC TV programme about boats from the period. As well as lifting the title twice in three years (coming second in the other season) and lifting the European Cup Winners' Cup, our team also reached three consecutive FA Cup finals, taking the trophy home once. Contained therein are games, performances, incidents and goals that I can recall with clarity to this day. To paraphrase Dickens, "It was the best of times. It was the worst of times…"

These days, I am a middle-aged man and not currently in a relationship, thus spend my time watching the Toffees home and away every week. Usually, my team flirts between average and chronic yet I continue to attend despite not being in love with the modern game nor its peripheral influences. I despair of it in fact, yet my ardour for my club and a match day with my mates stems back to my memories as much as it has anything to do with our current league status or player roster. Football then was a much harsher environment. Harder for both players and fans alike, whilst we, in transit and in the ground itself, were often treated no better than animals and were paying for the privilege. Yet I wouldn't swap my experiences for that of today's youth. Ours were loud, visceral, intense and sometimes even violent. Theirs are sanitised, choreographed, recorded and expensive.

This brief compilation has illuminated memories I hadn't considered for a while and for that I am grateful. But on a wider point, the experiences that will be listed by contributors will vary wildly yet I suspect they will all encapsulate a visceral connection with their club that I do not believe exists today. At least not in the same way. Apart from away tickets and travel, we could never really accuse our teams of fleecing us. Of just seeing us as marketing opportunities. They understood that we were here for the long haul. Now, they simply do not care.

Like I said, in a straight choice, I'd go for our option every time.

Brett T – West Ham

When I was younger, and now, I felt a bit of a loner. I started going to West Ham when I was seven. My dad too. No seats, just standing. I remember getting passed down the front over the top of everyone's heads, and planted on the wall before the pitch, until the steward would come along and get you down. This was the West side. I used to listen to the chants and banter and tried to copy them, but my hearing wasn't always in the right place, and I'd get them wrong. Yet I always looked forward to every home match. I looked over to the South Bank and saw some kids from my school. I started to go with them, meeting up before heading off to the match.

We were playing a team. I think it may have been Forest or Bristol City. Back in the day, you could pay and get in the ground anywhere. There was a shout that went up and a mass fight broke out. I stood there just watching, I was about ten or eleven years old and caught a smack in the head. I was stunned and hurt. When I looked up, my friend had disappeared. There were other West Hams fighting away and I remember being dragged out the way by a fellow Hammer. I don't know who he was, but I remembered him saying well done for standing there. He obviously saw something else other than me stunned.

I subsequently went to West Ham on my own for the rest of the season; the so-called friends having left me. But I found myself actively looking for these West Ham guys, with a feeling inside of me getting more and more. I wanted to be one of them, but one of what I did not know.

I finally identified the guy who pulled me out of the way and realised that he was one of the leaders of many firms who were over West Ham at the time. I lived a secret life of wanting to be one of them every day: school, judo and family life. I got the buzz, the adrenaline of being one of the lads.

Then I quickly started to go to away games and met more people, got more buzz and more adrenaline. Then I was going to every game. I loved the feeling of being wanted, and belonging to something that was bigger than anything I could think of at the time. Being a loner at the beginning and sometimes feeling on your own is a sad feeling and then before you know it, I was going to a Sunderland night match, losing 3-0 or on a Saturday 6-0. Playing football on the beach was a memory that you don't forget, like going to a European Championship final in Belgium, looking behind at all the other coaches knowing it's full of West Ham fans, brothers.

There was a darker side to football and I loved every minute of it. I wouldn't change anything. I have been to some places, seen and done some horrific things, that no one will know unless they were there. I look back and think, *How the f*** could we do these things?* But they were done.

The violence suddenly changed into not so much violence, but fun. The fighting gradually calmed down more and more over the years. It wasn't that we didn't want it, but we didn't go hunting for it as in the past. If it was there, we were up for it. When I was young, slightly older or even now, I still have that feeling we're invincible.

Having renewed, the first time I got my season ticket for the Olympic stadium in what is now called the Billy Bond's stand, I didn't know who was sitting either side of me. I arrived at the first game, went to my seat and there was a fella sitting in it. I said, "You're in my seat."

He said, "Yes, is it possible I can swap?" His seat was next to mine but his brother-in-law was on the other side. As a good West Ham fan, I said, "No probs, mate." We have been West Ham friends ever since. The man and his son next to me, the guy and his daughter behind us. Then some old friends two rows in front. That is the thing about my team. The way I look at it, I always had this motto, a belief that it doesn't matter if you have three eyes, walk funny, look like the way you are – if you're a West Ham fan, you're one of us and you should automatically get the protection of the pack or at least comfort from a fellow Hammer.

There is probably more to tell, but all I will say is it was the feeling of belonging, adrenaline and excitement. The feeling of being scared, and the general sense of holy f***, how did that happen? Being a West Ham supporter, we don't support them for being champs or winning everything as we don't. But win, lose or draw, it's family, it's life, it's what governed me.

John C – West Ham

I was born in Bromley-by-Bow in 1968 and spent my early years in Romford, before moving to Clacton when I was ten. My uncle went everywhere with West Ham in the 70s and had a fine collection of opposition fans' silk scarves taken as trophies. It was him who first took me to Upton Park, a 5-0 win over Newcastle in '79. I was hooked and started going to every home game, standing in the Chicken run where he would point out the faces in the TBF to me. I was always fascinated by the chanting and fights in the South Bank and by the age of thirteen, me and a mate I grew up with in Romford were standing there ourselves in our MA-1 Flight jackets.

Soon, through my parents, I met a London family in Clacton, the Gills. Their son Billy was a bit older than me but I started going to the football with him. He used to knock about with Kerry T and was, I think, related to one of the Chads, Dave M, so I was soon knocking about with some right faces.

I was soon fully into the way of life. All my money went on travelling around the country following the Hammers and on designer clothes. I loved everything about it. They were great days. Sadly, the game has changed and money has taken over. I still make the occasional trip over to Stratford for a few beers but that's it. I have great memories and have made great friends and if I could turn the clock back, I'd do it all again.

Bill R – Preston

Typing these notes up in 2020 during lockdown because of the world pandemic COVID-19, I'm going to be reminiscing about some of the decent clobber I've worn on match days to nigh on every league ground in England, and beyond. Plus some of the antics I got up to. Yet I'm sitting here in a scruffy, fence paint splattered T-shirt and jogging bottoms. Very unkempt for a fella in his mid-fifties that has spent a fortune on dressing the part since my teens, indeed. And the antics I'm up to at present are, walking the dog daily for my hour of exercise, while also catching up on the backlog of DIY I've been putting off for several years. This is due to still attending football, and going to the pub most weekends.

Over four decades, I've amassed almost one hundred coats and over fifty pairs of shoes and trainers, plus racks of shirts. I'm not a collector, I wear them. Though my missus says I've got OCD when it comes to what's in my wardrobes. Who am I to disagree? As for shenanigans, well, there's a book full, but don't tell the other half.

Growing up in a northern outpost, Preston, a child of the mind-bending 60s, fashion wasn't at the forefront when rolling around, scuffling with latchkey council kids on the front green – all while dodging broken bottles and white dog sh**e. But, dressing right and fashion did become a rite of passage once you started school, and noticing what boys of the same age were wearing. Even more so, when on parade at football strutting your stuff, peacock mode. Dressing the bollocks, as they say down south.

I was the third child to be born in the family, and the last, to parents of a defined age. They had married between the World Wars, and my father had served in the Royal Navy during WWII. My mother fell pregnant with their first child before my dad went back to war following a period of leave. When my dad returned home, my brother was nearly two years old. And now we moan when we can't get a signal on our phones or connect to the internet. Fashion to my parents meant smart clothes, not trendy clobber. I even had a side parting, when all the other boys had fringes (at fifteen, I once again had a side parting, only by choice then).

You might get the notion I wasn't dressed in the latest styles or trends at this time, in the late 60s and early 70s. This led to fights with other urchins who took the piss out of what I'd assembled. I wouldn't take no s**t. This followed two fights with brothers on the estate where we lived. I came in the house feeling sorry for myself after the altercations. I'd lost the second fight to the older brother of the first boy I fought. I was told by my dad, in no uncertain terms, to get back out and hit the older brother harder this time. My dad hated bullies, something that he instilled in me too, as well as morals.

A few years later, the two brothers had given a mouthful of grief to my mum. Upon this, my dad had a word with the pair about their manners. On hearing this, their dad staggered round to ours when he came back from his Sunday dinner time session, and offered my dad out – the mouthpieces must have gone squealing to daddy. I'd never seen my dad lift a finger in anger, or even raise his voice in rage. On hearing the challenge, my dad rolled up his shirt sleeves, and took a stance on our front lawn. The lads' dad turned, and did a walk of shame, even though he must have had twenty years on my dad. This was noted by me for future reference – show bottle and those of a certain kind will crumble.

Clocking what others were donning rather than what I was wrapped in, I began dogging my mum for certain items of "fashion". Prestige 70s items such as a green canvas parka with red lining and real rabbit fur trimming around the hood. Birmingham and Oxford bags – colossal waistbands with an excess of buttons, the wider the better. Platform shoes – elevation crucial. Even accessories played a part, like the right belt. There was an endless amount of dodgy fashion rigouts during the 70s which I could waffle on about. It was only in the late 70s when I discovered my first love: music. Namely punk. Yes, I went through a stage of dressing the part as a punk too. This morphed into skinhead in the latter part of the decade with the pristine smartness of Ben Sherman and Sta Press.

Come 1980, I'd began getting involved on match days. As in, getting stuck into the opposition and rival fans. The team in question, my hometown team: Preston North End. Turning fifteen, with brass in my pocket from a few part time jobs, I was also going out drinking of a weekend with lads who were a few years older than myself. This meant dressing smart to gain entry to certain pubs in town. Some of these lads were into northern soul. The soul boy scene was, and still is, big in the north. Wedge haircuts, burgundy tops, straight leg jeans and slip-on boat shoes being the look amongst the ranks. It was around this time I took in what lads, who followed other clubs from the north west, (how dare you) both Manc and Scouse teams, were wearing. This would be on Saturday nights, on returning from the games that they had attended that day. This was a lean towards sportswear. I once got called a "Manc twat" when flanking an escort of Bolton along Deepdale Road heading towards the ground. I was wearing a pink Fila T-shirt, yellow Sergio Tacchini bottoms (both purchased in Manchester the week before) and a pair of Nike Wimbledons.

At this stage, nobody had a name for the phenomenon that would be classed as casual or dresser. The lads I knocked about with had an eclectic taste in genres of music. Morphing from a variety of punks, skins, mods, soul boys, scooter boys and older boot boys, etc. A new look began to take shape on the terraces of Deepdale – North End's ground – and right across the UK. As much as watching the field of play, I'd look around me to see what other labels the lads were wearing, even more so what those in the away end were wearing. Or I would scan the side terracing and seats at away games. It was hard to make out what other lads had on when you were chasing them down the street with only the soles of their trainers to be seen, or when being chased yourself.

The first label to have was Slazenger, and their jumpers – a label laughed at nowadays. I had a few gold panther embossed Slazie jumpers in different colours. Le Coq Sportif cycling, or skiing tops were worn underneath. I could just about squeeze in to the largest youth size at fifteen, which were a couple of quid cheaper too. It was hard work to acquire the jumpers in the two shops in Preston that stocked Slazies. Unlike the Levi cords and jeans to go with them. There was an Army & Navy store that had a vast shop floor with a bounty of circular rails and others fixed to the walls. I would wait until someone had the shop assistant's attention, hold aloft a pair of 30-32" cords on a hanger – I'd slipped two pairs on the hanger – and ask if I could try them on in the changing room. I would then quickly put on a pair of the cords under the jeans I was wearing, pull back the curtain on the changing room, announce they weren't to my taste, and then do one, rapid. Oh the days before security tags. Footwear was Adidas, Kick or red Kicker shoes to go out on the town.

Shopping or robbing became commonplace to look the part. Though it wasn't like today's environment, when most labels are stocked in one vast boutique, or the click of a button away on the internet. Golf, tennis, and men's outfitters would be sought out. You had to rely on ITK lads or unearth a goldmine in your own neck of the woods yourself. If not, jumping on the rattler to Manchester came a regular occurrence with the mecca that was Hurley's. Top of the list. This, after trekking across the city centre. Sportswear would be dripping from the shop's high ceiling out of shoplifters' reach. Wonderous tracksuit tops hung on hooks like grand stalactites to feast your eyes on. Liverpool had Wade Smith's, to procure trainers brought over in the back of a Transit van from Germany. Or out of scallies' Adidas holdalls that had been grafting round Europe, on a rubbed out Transalpino ticket. Such footwear from the shopping trips was then acquired by the shop's owner, Wade Smith, and sold on to eager punters.

In the two cities mentioned, you had to be wary and have your wits about you. It didn't matter if it wasn't a match day. Many a time you had to be on your toes or you might be robbed of your wares. There were always plenty of shady characters hanging around to relieve you of your purchase. The odd time London was paid a visit too. Even on my own doorstep there was a select sprinkling of outlets. I was once closely followed around a tennis wear establishment by an assistant. On asking if they stocked any characteristic tennis labels, I was versed that folk from Liverpool had either cut off all the badges on such items or stolen them. The other shops in Preston had the odd commodity though. Gibson's was Preston's version of Hurley's/ Wade Smith's. Gibson's was steamed and emptied by likeminded lads from opposing teams arriving by train in Preston and stumbling upon the shop on multiple occasions.

Over the next few years, labels came and went at the blink of an eye. Some of my clobber wouldn't last long. Not due to the fact of what was in and what was out, but because endless togs became casualties at the match. A yellow Pringle jumper became unwearable after running through a "wall of death" in the seats at Deepdale – Pompey always made a show. I more or less ripped the red and white collar off a dark blue Fila polo from vaulting over the turnstiles to save the entrance fee at Deepdale once. I lost a Puma California trainer during the stampede down the stairs of the stands at

Deepdale too. This was while fleeing a baying mob of DLF, that more than outnumbered us. When both firms stood to face each other in the car park outside the ground, the California was returned with pinpoint accuracy between my eyes by a Derby lad. It was pulled on speedily as we made a tactical retreat – the DLF were on top form that day.

As mentioned, an early footwear of choice was Kickers. I have both fond and bad memories of the shoe. This is because I was on the receiving end of the soles of a pair of Kickers one sunny afternoon on the first home game of the season, in the form of a Millwall lad dancing on my head after falling over during an intense ruck. Then there was a grail of a white, Lacoste baseball cap, with a green sun visor peak and large crocodile on the front. I jibbed college one day, where I was attending a bricklaying apprenticeship, and caught the rattler to Manchester, before heading to Hurley's – an Aladdin's cave for a casual/dresser back then. The whole day is a story in itself. But to cut to the chase, Rochdale's striker lashed the ball wide of Preston's goalmouth at Spotland, Rochdale's ground, and it was heading in my direction. I stuck my nut out, and headed the ball back to the field of play. Only I forgot I had the Lacoste hat that I'd purchased that morning.

That was the end of it, now with a crumbled peak, never to be worn again. A police dog once liked the leg of a pair of Levi jeans I was wearing. The snarling mutt liked them so much, it ragged the left leg off them. A classic Robe di Kappa jumper was stretched to three sizes bigger against Millwall in a vicious brawl – not the Kicker incident – on the streets leading to Deepdale. You lose some, you win some. And I defo lost that one...

The one I was most gutted about was an Ellesse ski jacket that got slashed down the back a few times while on Burnley's ground, Turf Moor. It wasn't even at a game versus Preston. It was a match when Burnley entertained Wigan and ten of us had gone for our football violence fix. Other items had to be binned or worn for graft after being covered in claret. There were plenty of other misfortunes while participating in fisticuffs and skulduggery to my togs. Yes plenty.

The next phase, especially in the north, was the dressing down period. Tweed jackets, cord or denim Levi shirts. Cord or Clarks shoes. And flares. Flares varied in width depending on taste or whether you had a lean towards the Manc or Scouse outlook on the take. This rigout was the opposite to what every dog and its owner was wearing when finally latching onto a casual/dresser look. The dressing down/scruff look was a total backlash to preference of bright colours and pastel shades sportswear. Then came the rambler phase: Berghaus jackets, baggy jeans and walking boots. Next up, Paninaro, the Italian youthful style of dressing. Bubble jackets, big logoed sweatshirts and Timberland shoes. And as the rave scene took a grip of some football lads and being "loved-up", they didn't bother so much about what they wore, or fighting. This is when others went down the road of the £500 plus jackets. The desired labels being Stone Island, CP Company and anything Massimo Osti put his name to.

In just over ten years, designer labels had gone from being seen and just worn by elitists, to being donned by lads in pubs and sat in the seats at the match. Yes, football lads had created what is classed as fashion without even knowing or wanting too. Then with the calm of acid and E waning, the English disease reared its ugly head once more making a comeback, after a hazy lull. Only by now the police had CCTV, plus other ways and means of stopping boys being boys. But mobile phones soon arranged meets far away from prying eyes. Today, the match day experience can be sterile, including on the pitch, and violence is rare.

I personally have been through all these junctures. I've worn the threads, and travelled by a varied means of transport doing so to watch my team. Planes, trains and automobiles. Clapped-out trains that had rammed compartments with lads under the seats, on luggage racks or hid in the bogs, jibbing. Buses with a bucket to piss in and twice the amount that should be aboard with enough ale to sink a ship. Transit vans holding world records for the amount they fitted in. Cars that weren't taxed, insured or even owned by the driver were used as modes to get to the four corners of the UK. I would do this with mates made for life. Lads who I met on the dilapidated stands of Deepdale, or had my back in chaotic street fights. Lads I've shared many a pint and laugh with, plus trips abroad. Lads that I've been to their weddings, their offspring's christenings and their children's weddings and christenings. More sadly, too many good lads' funerals whose lives have been taken far too early – RIP North Enders in the sky. The bond of football, fighting and just being there in the moment comes second to none – apart from my son's birth, that is.

But right through these eras of casual/dresser, I was, and still am, a football fan. A football fan that loves watching football live. A football fan that has spent thousands of pounds watching my team, and England too, over land and sea. A football fan that has stood on windswept terraces in the pouring rain, soaked through to the bone on a Wednesday night in November, over 200 miles from home. A football fan that has spent a week away on foreign shores in the baking sun, for ninety minutes of football, where the locals make you as unwelcome as possible – mad dogs and English men. A football fan that has been elated to the brink of tears of joy. A football fan that has had to hide tears of despair. Yes, the highs and lows of being a football fan, that only a football fan would put themselves through.

Only following Preston North End from the mid-70s onwards, there haven't been many highs. PNE have the prestige accolade of being the first double winners in the first season of any sort of football league and Cup competition, being a founder member of the league in 1888. They didn't even concede in the Cup, and were nicknamed the original Invincibles. North End's ground is the oldest football ground to stage major league football. The legendary Tom Finney spent all his career playing for Preston too. Having won several trophies over the years, in my time these trophies have been few and far between. Spiralling out of Division 2 at the beginning of the 80s, by the year 1986, proud Preston had to apply for re-election to secure league status after finishing ninety-first in the basement fourth league. The famous club had no finances, no floodlights – fans were shaking tins outside the ground for funds to pay for new floodlights – and no crowd: less than 3000 sometimes. I kept on going to games, it was in my blood.

Promotions and relegations have happened during my term of support. Two play-off finals to reach the promised land have ended in more heartache. Preston have been involved in more play-offs than any other team. North End now has four new stands, an owner that is in the top thirty rich list, and a decent team and manager while sitting pretty in the Championship at this moment. But who knows what will happen with all football on hold in 2020?

Nowadays, I'm friends with lads from all over the country from other clubs. Trips abroad following England, you make friendships with old rivals when every local wants an English scalp. We swap tales of the golden age, and reminisce of battles many moons gone. Sometimes I will go to one of their fixtures, or they come to one of Preston's. Mutual respect for those that have been there, done that and got the T-shirt. Though there are some teams I'm still not welcomed by with open arms. The Old Bill takes a second look and can't get their heads round us being buddies, for some reason.

I think the majority of football lads through the years are very much alike. Unequivocal standards and a way of addressing oneself. It's just that we followed different teams. You might even get a certain glance and sometimes a knowing nod when in a pub or walking to the ground off of lads you don't know. They just know, and you know too. It's the way you carry yourself. It's the item of clobber not known to the untrained eye. It's the small lapel badge stating who you follow, rather than singing aloud and making yourself known or by wearing a replica shirt.

Would I change things? Regrets, I have a few, but... who doesn't? No, once in, never out, only the boxing gloves are hung up, and the football is key. Well, apart from the match banter with the lads, a decent pint of real ale and observing any aggro, from afar... *wink*

William Routledge; author of *Northern Monkeys* and *Oh Yes, Oh Yes, We Are the PPS.*

Brenden Wyatt "Jockey" – Liverpool

People get asked, "What are your first memories of going to the match?" or "When did you get involved with the casual/terrace culture?"

For me, it was a bit different. I was born on the Kirkdale side of Everton Valley in 1966, so my first memories quite often involved football crowds and violence. Anyone who's ever visited Anfield or Goodison will be familiar with Everton Valley as it's the main thoroughfare to both grounds if you've arrived at Lime Street. Many firms will testify to coming unstuck around those streets. So, from around about the age of three or four (in 1970) I would see firms like Forest, Chelsea, Leeds and of course Man United's Red Army arriving en masse on my doorstep to cause mayhem... and I loved every f***ing minute of it.

For us, Goodison and Anfield were our playgrounds. We lived a five-minute walk from both, and as we got older it would be Liverpool one week, Everton the next for the young scallies from our area. I remember the summer of 1971 and the talk all week was about the Red Army coming to town... we knew it wasn't the Russians but a boot boy army from Manchester. We'd heard our parents talking about shops boarding their windows up because of this notorious horde.

It was a Friday in August when they came and I was making plans for the evening ahead, minding cars like we normally did for all games when they started arriving mid-afternoon. They looked as scary as the reputation that preceded them with their denim jackets, jeans half way up their legs and eighteen-hole oxblood Doc Martens. I've missed out a very important detail. They hadn't come to face Everton or Liverpool. They were playing a home game at Anfield against Arsenal, as crowd violence had seen them banned from playing home games at Old Trafford.

They started arriving mid-afternoon and the Scouse bizzies were right on them, taking the laces out of their boots, making it difficult for them to run riot. I didn't venture up to the ground as I was only five but I remember the running battles outside our house. Everton and Liverpool skins had joined forces to welcome them. It was terrifying and exciting in equal measure... I was hooked.

So, it was against this backdrop that I started taking an interest in more than what was happening on the pitch. I went to my first game aged seven, at Anfield with my mate, but we didn't have a responsible adult with us. We were minding cars and then just followed the crowds up to the Spoon Kop and bunked in under the turnstiles. Today, looking back, I can still smell the aroma of chip paper, piss and then turf as we got onto the famous terrace. We were playing Leicester and I don't remember the score. That was irrelevant. It was the beginning of a journey that would see me watch my team in thirty-six countries and serve three foreign jail sentences.

To become a Kopite, you had to serve an apprenticeship in the Old Boys' Pen, stuck in the top right-hand corner of the old Kop. It was a tough place to learn your trade and was inhabited by gangs of kids from all of the toughest areas of Liverpool. I'm still mates with some of the kids I first met there over four decades ago. But we were a different breed than our older brothers and when it was time to move on to the Kop, we didn't. Instead, we headed down to the other end of the ground and by the age of twelve, I was a fully paid-up member of the Annie Road end crew.

This would have been around 1978. My balls were dropping and I was out looking for adventure.

Liverpool were cementing themselves as the kings of Europe and looking back, both Liverpool and Everton had a huge following of young lads around my age. Scouse football firms were changing. Out had gone the check shirted, long-haired, scarf-wearing groups of the 70s. Something was happening on the streets and terraces of Merseyside. The city's two teams were forming two scally armies with their own look, outlook and attitude. Punk had emerged a couple of years earlier and it started to integrate itself into mainstream youth culture just as the skins and mods had influenced us. It was a great fusion also mixed with a bit of Bowie and Roxy Music.

So, around the early part of 1978, it was out with the flares and in with the likes of drainpipe jeans, Slazenger or Fred Perry jumpers and Adidas Samba or Stan Smith. Around that period, the jeans were changing monthly. It could be Lois one week then Inega or Ritzy, Fiorucci or Fu's. Fu's at that time could at first only be bought at the Jean Machine in Manchester's Arndale – it was like an away match going to buy them as the Mancs would know we were coming and wait in little gangs around the Arndale. But still we went... f***ing madness. Tell that to the Clone Island firm who do their shopping on their phones nowadays.

Music played a big part in the development. David Bowie had recently released his Berlin phase Low album and young Scousers adopted the wedge style haircut sported by him on the album cover. The sportswear didn't really come into play 'till around 1981 and no one would really argue against the Scousers having the upper hand, again due to our excursions into Europe closely followed by the Mancs. No disrespect to the Cockneys (all Londoners are Cockneys to us) but the London clubs mostly seemed to be skinhead firms 'till around 1982, maybe a bit earlier. I know they had their soul boys but the main firms coming to Anfield and Goodison in the '81-'82 season were all wearing green flying jackets. They soon got their game together and were wearing a uniform of Pringle, Farah and Gabicci. All the London clubs used to turn up on Merseyside. In my view, Arsenal were the best dressed, West Ham the most organised, Chelsea and Spurs equally respected. You had to have your wits about you when you visited all the London gaffs.

So, we had started venturing into Europe in the early 80s and there were easy pickings to be had. Sportswear on the continent back then was sold mainly to sportsmen and wasn't really recognised as a fashion accessory, until we arrived. The big sports brands wouldn't supply the UK market as they could see we were in a recession and thought it was a non-starter. You could only really get the likes of Samba, Mamba, Kick, Gazelle, Nastasie and the like. Next thing you know, we'd return with Trimm Trabs, Grand Slams and much more. It didn't just stop at Adidas. These were the golden years of tennis and some of the gear back then was bang on. Fila and Tacchini, to name just two, had been sported on centre court by Borg and McEnroe, and were soon on the backs of young Scousers who'd never lifted a tennis racquet in their lives.

At first, the football facilitated these trips but in the end, we were going even when there wasn't a game on. It wasn't always plain sailing. We would be hopping around Europe on Transalpino or Interrail tickets in the early days. You could buy a Transalpino ticket from London to Ostend for £11.50 but with the help of an ink rubber or brake fluid, the ticket could be doctored, and the destination changed to Vienna. The beauty of it was that you could add a "via" in and go via somewhere else. There were times when we'd arrive at a German town or city and bump into another Scouse firm (even when there wasn't a game on) and we'd decide to get back on the train as that town was now probably on top. We also arrived at train stations to discover graffiti stating, "Hard luck, Scousers. Cockneys beat you to it!"

Once, three of us were sitting on a train at Ostend, then saw a group heading down the platform. As they got alongside us, we realised they were Mancs, and they recognised us. We bolted further up the train away from them and ended up locking ourselves in the bog. They were about sixty handed. We didn't know there was a game on, but it turned out they were playing in Köln. For about an hour, they tried to get into the bog and even used one of the emergency hammers to gain entry. By the time the plod got on at Aachen and rescued us, there was a hole nearly half a foot wide in the door. Many years later, I'd share a joke with some of the Mancs who were there that day.

We were the second generation of scallies. In 1981, I was only fifteen and although we were getting up to all kinds, there had been older lads than us that had been doing it a while longer. Taking a look at the pictures the likes of Mono has and it shows the evolution: in 1977, flares and snorkels, to only a few months later heading into 1978 and they're wearing drainpipe jeans and Adidas (they'd "picked up" in Germany) and on and on towards 1980. The hair, jackets and clothing had morphed into the finished article which in my view is still adopted by some to this day.

Firms older than us had been heading to the continent for a few years due to Liverpool's involvement in European competitions, the likes of the Huyton Baddies and the Scotty Road firm had been the bane of continental jewellery shops for a while by the time we started bringing the sportswear home. A football game was always a great excuse for a bit of graft. I remember when we played in Austria in the 80s and during the game, there was a regular group of sportswear and jewellery shop owners walking 'round the running track accompanied by police trying to pick out spectators in the Liverpool end who may have made a visit to their store earlier in the day. Everyone was wrapped up in bubble coats and ski hats to deal with the cold Tyrol weather, of course.

A good mate of mine who's no longer with us, "Boylo", was grafting in Europe with the older kids when he was still in school. He was in my class and arguably one of the first to constantly bring the gear back when sportswear became the uniform of choice. If you wanted to know what the latest trainers or trackies were, then you headed up the Anfield Road on a Saturday afternoon and saw what Boylo was wearing after one of his trips abroad. He'd be finished with it a week or so later and that item would probably see another two or three owners such was the upmanship and speed the fashion changed.

Most of us served continental jail sentences. It was an occupational hazard. I remember whilst doing a stretch in Stadelheim Prison, Munich (Hitler had been a previous guest there), I asked for an English book from the library. Inside the pages would be messages of previous readers: "BINNSY MUFC", "GOONERS", "YIDS" and "EFC, SCOUSERS RULE".

I'd bump into all kinds of firms back then, even Scouse firms we didn't know. Besides Cockneys and Mancs, grafters from Blackburn and Leeds, there was even a firm from Naples who were up to the same as us. I honestly believe that all the kids mentioned above influenced the direction fashion went in this country, whether they were from Collyhurst, the council estates of London or the terraces of Merseyside, they all played their bit.

Rob D – Bournemouth/Man U

The beginning of the casual scene.

Some of you reading this may have read my book *No Ticket Required*, which concentrates on my time following Manchester United and the various scams we used to gain free entrance, travel, accommodation etc. I was born and raised in Bournemouth and so have supported them all my life. I also followed a big team (Manchester United) as many lads down here do. This was mainly on the back of watching my first FA Cup final on TV in 1977. It was the late 80s when I started to follow United on a regular basis, so the following covers the years before this with AFC Bournemouth – when I became a casual.

As teenagers still at school, we were a mixed bunch fashion-wise in the early 80s. My favourite music was punk, so I wore black jeans, a Clash or Siouxie Soux and the Banshees T-shirt and a few other odd bits of clothing. The rest of the lads were influenced more by the skinhead or two-tone look with DMs, Sta Press trousers, Fred Perry polos, green Flight jackets, Harrington jackets etc. We were a mishmash of styles but come match day, we united. Home games, meet at Jumpers Common and walk to the match. Away games, meet at Jumpers Common and crowd around a radio to listen to the match with a bottle of Merrydown cider. It was 1982 when I first heard boys at school talking about Fila and Tacchini, and other exotic labels. Literally speaking, about three boys started to wear a few bits to school.

I left school in 1983 and that summer set about sorting some decent clobber. Leo Leisurewear in the Boscombe Arcade stocked some decent bits and also some crap (Leo Gemelli). Come on, we all had one. I remember always peering in the window before heading to the Academy under-18s disco. Austin Reed on Westover Road had a decent sports section downstairs with plenty of Fila and Ellesse. The golf shop in Lower Parkstone stocked Pringle and Lyle & Scott, and Benetton had a shop in town. Flix in Christchurch was also good for a smart jumper that you could get away with on the terraces. The younger ones amongst our group embraced this look first, while the older lads were still more skinhead in appearance, wearing sheepskins or s**t leather jackets. I say the older lads, they were still under twenty!

Here's a summary of the most worn items or brands. Footwear: Adidas trainers, Gazelles, Samba, Grand Prix, Trimm Trab, Ivan Lendl and München were popular, along with Diodora Borg, Puma G Vilas and Kicker boots with the little leather tag. We had a spell of wearing these tags on our trainers, lads used to nick them from shops. Trousers: split and frayed jeans, Farah's, Lois or Benetton jumbo cords. Tops: a polo or tennis shirt, anything which was worn at Wimbledon would do. Paisley shirts were also a good look on the terraces or in a club. Tracksuit tops: Fila, Sergio Tacchini, Kappa or Ellesse. Jumpers: Braemar, Lyle & Scott, Pierre Cardin and Giorgio Armani were popular, with Pringle being the most worn. Coats: Patrick or Adidas raincoats, or a ski coat for when it got cold. Ellesse and Kappa were also popular. Jackets made with sections of leather and material with a hood were also decent.

By 1984, there were a good twenty of us from Christchurch all looking the part and probably another twenty or so well-dressed Bournemouth lads, with a few others from Parkstone making up AFC Bournemouth's casuals. The home end was the South End and we often arrived late so we could all walk up the tunnel together chanting, "Christchurch boys, we are here." We liked being different and standing out in our brightly coloured attire. The rest of the South End was a mixture of skinheads, mods, rockabillies, the odd teddy boy and scarfers in snorkel coats and Y cardigans. You also had the trendies who looked like extras from a Duran Duran video. We would often bump into rival mobs and many a skirmish occurred on the cricket pitch next to Dean Court, or in the side streets off Windham Road, where away fans would take a short cut up from Bournemouth train station.

We were in the fourth division and our rivals were the Bristol clubs, Aldershot, Reading, Pompey, Brentford, Gillingham, Swansea, Newport and Exeter. These were the games we would take better numbers to as they weren't that far away. We'd get the train but the police could easily keep an eye on us so cars and Transit vans became the preferred method of transport. Away days in the 80s with a small club like Bournemouth could be dodgy as we were usually heavily outnumbered. A few of the lads would come and not even go to the games, preferring to relieve the local arcade fruit machines via the art of "strimming".

We were, as mentioned, a mixed bag. Some of us loved the football and the clothes, some loved fighting and a few had more criminal leanings. The cricket pavilion in Kings Park near to the ground served beer and they kept barrels in the cellar. Before one home game, we broke in, and with a car parked outside, proceeded to lift a barrel of beer. Whilst this was happening, a mob from the away team turned up and off it went. A battle was going on all around whilst four of us were rolling the beer barrel to the car. There was a cricket match taking place and the fighting spilled onto the pitch with stumps being pulled up and used as weapons. The cricketers weren't happy and the whole incident made the local paper. No idea who won the fight or the match but we all enjoyed free beer that night!

These were the days when we would occasionally go into the away end at Dean Court in ones and twos and then all meet up and give it a burst of "Bournemouth", resulting in a brief skirmish before the police would kick a few out or usually just walk us down the pitch and put us back in the South End. I can remember full pitch invasions during matches, with both ends going on and charging up and down the field. As a nipper, this was so exciting. More often than not, very few punches were landed, but the fact you were able to jump over the barriers and run down the pitch gave such a buzz.

The clothes changed fast with various items coming and going at an alarming pace. I remember us all wearing tweed hats once to Arsenal in the Cup in the late 80s. The leather patch jackets (Poachers) came and went. The carrying of an umbrella was the done thing for a while or having a newspaper in your back pocket also. We called it a Millwall brick. All the top clothes cost a fortune back then. In 1984, I paid £55 for a Sergio Tacchini Orion tracksuit top from Nik Naks in London. An equivalent would cost the same now, but wages are maybe ten times higher now; basically, a tracksuit top cost about £550 in today's terms.

Different regions had different looks and I remember the Midlands clubs turning up in flares one season when we were all wearing straight jeans. Bristol City had a big mob all wearing green Barbour wax jackets. The biggest shock was when Bournemouth got promoted to the old Division 2 in the late 80s. We were used to a few hundred away fans tops, with the casual element being maybe thirty or so lads. All of a sudden, clubs like Blackburn and Leicester, who we all thought would be farmers, arrived with loads of well-dressed lads and caused us loads of bother. Derby brought a couple of thousand and must have had at least five or six hundred casuals. We got run everywhere.

Apart from the Bournemouth shops, we would also travel to Southampton, but London was the place then if you were serious about your clobber. My beloved Tacchini tracksuit top met an untimely death around 1987. Was it ripped off me in a terrace scuffle? Was I taxed for this stylish clobber? No, I was cycling to town with it tied around my waist and it slipped down and my back cog ripped a row of oily holes straight down my top. I was gutted but it was probably time to move on. It was also probably time to think about buying a car but all my money went on clothes, Benson & Hedges and beer. All the local lads who had a car and drove around Westover Road dressed like Wurzel Gummidge, scruffy twats. They all seemed to have a girlfriend though, although we did all right on that score – even with our permed at the back hair! Charlie Nicholas has a lot to answer for.

The classic casual or tennis look had moved on and I was now wearing Chipie, Chevignon, Classix Nouveaux, Marco Polo, Ocean Pacific and other such labels. To me, the classic casual look would be a pair of Gazelles, Lois cords, a Lacoste polo, round neck Pringle jumper and an Aquascutum scarf. Hey, I'm no style leader and

Bournemouth was years behind Liverpool, Manchester, London etc. but these were brilliant times and probably the last major youth culture in Britain. Britpop in the 90s was great because I loved the music and could still wear Gazelles and a Lacoste polo and fit in.

It's now 2021 and guess what I'm still wearing? Keep it casual, lads.

German Martin – West Ham

You could tell from a very young age that football was for me. Before I went to school, I could already write one word. Well, it wasn't exactly a word but more like 3 letters put together: VfB. It is the name of the local football club in Stuttgart and stands for "Verein für Bewegungspiele". Now try to pronounce that, my English friends! The love for my club was, of course, installed in me by my dad. Apparently, while watching another game on TV, I asked him who was playing and if my hometown Stuttgart had such a team as well. Soon after that, my dad took me to my first football match. VfB Stuttgart were playing a team called Röchling Völklingen in the old second Bundesliga South. I still remember that day, I was only five years old. The flags, the colours, the noise, the celebrations as the goals went in. I was overwhelmed. Stuttgart won 4-3. Despite there only being 17,000 people in the Neckarstadion –

which had a capacity of 70,000 – the experience was incredible for me as a little boy. I wanted more.

Stuttgart won promotion back to the top flight in my first season as a supporter. That surely was a sign that VfB needed me. And I needed them. Going to games with my dad was always the highlight for me. We didn't have a season ticket but did go now and then, mainly when I was getting on my father's nerves too much. Saturday evenings were perfect when we won and extremely miserable when we lost. This was much to my mum's annoyance who couldn't understand how a simple game of twenty-two men chasing a ball had such an impact in my life.

As I was getting older, I went with some of my mates from school and my village. We graduated and finally were accepted to stand with the older hardcore fans in the so-called A-Block in the Neckarstadion, soon attending away games as well. This was the time my relationship with West Ham started.

In the late 70s and early 80s, only a few European matches were broadcast on TV. Needless to say, I watched them all even if it meant staying up 'till almost midnight and being tired the following day at school. When there was an English team involved, the atmosphere was something else. The grounds were tighter, the supporters closer to the pitch, there were no running tracks. The fans were singing, roaring, swaying and not just chanting the name of their team. There were no Kutten. For those of you not familiar with German football culture, this is a jean jacket with loads of badges sewn on.

I had to find a club in England to support, or even better, a club to find me! I've never been a glory hunter, so the obvious choice of Liverpool never appealed to me. Okay, they were on TV most often, had massive support but were just a bit like Bayern München at that time in Germany. Anyone could support a successful team. Nothing special about that. I did a lot of research in those days. I laid my hands on anything I could get about English football until only a handful of clubs were on my shortlist with West Ham being top. Why West Ham? For a start, I loved the colours. No German team played in claret and blue. I liked the name. Being a club from London, the travelling would be a bit easier. Plus, during my research, I learnt that West Ham had a bit of a reputation for playing nice football on the pitch and a reputation for looking after themselves off the pitch. I liked that. I won't mention the other clubs on the shortlist though. Just put it this way: I was young and didn't know better.

My plan stood: "When I'm old enough, I want to go to England and watch football there." Until then, I had to be content with what I was able to hear or read about West Ham. There was a radio show which reported the English Division 1 results via a telephone call by a guy named Arthur Rotmil from London, at five to six in the evening. So, after a home game in Stuttgart, I ran to the station, got on the first train back to my village and switched the radio on just in time to learn West Ham's result.

In those days, it was really hard to keep in touch. I was lucky enough to have a friend at school whose dad would spend the whole family holiday in a pub somewhere in Wales and serve behind the bar in exchange for free drinks, food and accommodation. He always brought football magazines, newspaper cuttings and other football related stuff from his holiday back to Germany. I then subscribed to a magazine called Shoot! I read about Frank McAvennie who soon became my favourite player. It was also West Ham's most successful season ever. The bond between West Ham and I got closer and closer. But it was still just theory. I had to wait another year when my parents finally let me go to London on my own.

It was during a school break in autumn that I boarded the train at one in the morning from Stuttgart Central station to Oostende which got me to Dover via the ferry, and then into London by teatime. I was accompanied by a friend who wasn't really into football, more culture. No problem, he went to museums and theatres, I went to football. We had a great time. I couldn't wait for the last day of our holiday. It was the big one: West Ham were playing Manchester United.

This was different from all the other football experiences I'd had so far. You could feel the hatred in the air the minute you got off the tube at Upton Park station. You could only see men aged fifteen to fifty-five, hardly any colours. Most shops were closed on Green Street. The atmosphere inside the ground was electric. I wished this game wouldn't end after ninety minutes. I wanted more. I still remember hearing the Bee Gees' "You Win Again" after the final whistle while I stood there promising myself to return.

I kept my promise whenever I had enough money to finance the trips. Flights were so expensive before the arrival of budget airlines. I often stayed in London for a few days when West Ham had a mid-week game, enabling me to watch a home and away game during my spell in England.

Being on my own, I had to be careful, especially at away games. During this time in the late 80s, I was advised to never make eye contact with anybody inside a pub. I didn't know the reason behind this but I followed the advice and I was okay. Apart from Middlesbrough away, when as usual I was standing by the bar minding my own business. A huge bloke came up to me and said straight away, "Who the fuck are you?" "Martin from Germany," I stuttered. Not being fully satisfied with my answer he went, "Who do you support?" I thought, *This is not looking good*. But being the honest person that I am replied, "West Ham." While I expected a punch in the teeth. This geezer said, "Right, I've seen you before over West Ham." He tested my allegiance by asking me several questions about our players, history and so on. Now this was easy for me as I was quite an anorak at that time, reading everything about West Ham I could get hold of. He then invited me over to the table where his friends were drinking, saying, "You stay with us. Middlesbrough is a rough place." I didn't need a tour guide to come to this obvious conclusion but I felt much safer within their group. These are some of the people who have become solid friends over the years.

As West Ham's hardcore support is very close knit, once you know the main people and are respected and accepted, you are part of the family. My days of being a loner were finally over. I could probably fill a whole book with the great times I've had following West Ham but I won't bore you to death.

I could go on about the pre-season friendlies abroad which are a right laugh. It's always the same people doing these trips. I've been to the USA, Canada, all over Europe with the Hammers in the company of life-long friends. You know who you are!

What makes West Ham special for me and sets us apart from all other clubs is that we are supported by real characters. I've often walked into a pub at away games and thought, *That geezer over there just looks West Ham*, without having seen him before. And almost every time I've been right.

West Ham is family. It's like a brother who lives abroad and you want to see each other as often as possible.

Tony Higgins – Newcastle

I was born in Newcastle-upon-Tyne in 1967, but grew up in the ship building town of Jarrow, six miles east along the River Tyne. The town is famous for the march to London in 1936. I loved football from a young age and remember Cup final day being the highlight of the year. I can still name all of the finals from about '73 to '80 and all the goal scorers etc. Things get a bit hazy after that.

Of course, as a kid, I was into all the things you now see on retro Facebook pages: the football cards with the appalling bubble gum, Panini stickers, Subbuteo, Super Striker and Wembley Trophy orange footballs. The latter we would kick from morning time until it got dark. That isn't romanticism either, that's how it was for me and my mates.

My old man wasn't really into football and had no interest in taking me to a match. His only interest in the game was the football pools, something he religiously played in the hope of winning his way out of the drudgery of a cold and wet Tyneside shipyard. I was taken to my first game by my mate's dad, a Newcastle United reserves match when I was about eight or nine. I have vivid memories of David Craig, the Northern Ireland international who was coming to the end of his career. A Fairs Cup winner with the club in 1969. I remember standing in the empty Leazes End. It looked colossal to my younger self. The Leazes End is part of Geordie folklore but unfortunately, I never witnessed it during a "real" game. Older mates are still full of stories on how it was mental and are adamant that the reason it was knocked down had nothing to do with redevelopment and more to do with it being literally un-policeable.

They have told me of skinheads having sex on the terraces with skin girls. When there wasn't a decent away mob, there were gang fights between the different areas of Tyneside. Added to that, there'd be the occasional huge bonfire lit in the middle of it. By the time I was regularly going to matches, the Leazes was a shadow of its former self and later housed the away supporters.

My hometown, Jarrow, is split seventy/thirty between Newcastle and Sunderland. I went to a few Sunderland games when I was eleven or so. That was around 1978 but in all honesty, music was starting to become more interesting to me by then, hand in hand with the associated fashion. Punk was still the thing in the north east at that time, with the Angelic Upstarts being the region's flagship band.

Cut to the back end of '79, I started to get into ska and what I perceived to be skinhead/rude boy bands such as The Specials and Madness. I loved the look of Fred Perry polos and Crombie coats. Soon after that, I was introduced to Oi! music by a mate who used to read Sounds music magazine religiously, and got introduced to bands like The 4 Skins, Last Resort and Infa Riot. Another band I loved were the Cockney Rejects. By this time, I was beginning to rekindle my interest in football, probably influenced by some of their lyrics.

Away from the north east, I had an auntie who lived in Waltham Abbey, on the Hertfordshire/Essex border, and every other summer, we would holiday there as a family. I loved it. On trips into London, I would spend more time reading the graffiti on the tube and in the train stations, than I would taking note of any famous monuments. One vibrant memory I have is of a group of Spurs skins getting on a Victoria line tube. One had a brown Harrington jacket. I hadn't seen before. London was always a bit of a magnet, to be honest.

I left school in '83 with scant qualifications. Historically, par for the course would have been to follow in the footsteps of my dad, both grandads and great grandads (and countless uncles and cousins) into the Tyneside shipyards. However, Margaret Thatcher and her Conservative government decided that ships could be built and purchased cheaper elsewhere. This meant that I spent one year on a YTS and then three and half years in a dead-end factory making kitchen worktops. Although the money was s**t, it was at this time I got into following Newcastle United all over the country. Needless to say, we were into all the scams of the day. Probably more out of necessity than anything else. We did the Persil train tickets and family railcards, but my favourite was the Mars bar wrappers for cheap coach tickets from Newcastle to London. There were two types of coach you could use them on: National Express or Clipper. The latter left from outside the Odeon Cinema, at the bottom of Northumberland Street. The coach would leave on a Friday at midnight and the routine was to meet in the Adelphi bar and have a couple of beers at last orders, before boarding for the long journey south.

A few times, the odd drunk individual got press ganged by us and ended up waking up at six in the morning, on the outskirts of London, still dressed in their Friday night going-out clothes. The coach would arrive at Victoria around seven and we would then make our way across to the markets around London Bridge, where the bars opened early for the stallholders and workers. From there, we would go to the West End, normally Soho, and end up congregating in the St. James Tavern (the name was the draw) before setting off to the various clubs across London. They were long days as we'd normally get the midnight coach back up north and not arrive home until six on the Sunday morning.

Regarding clobber, it's fair to say that fashion-wise we were a bit behind for the first few years of the casual scene, but there was a small group with wedges and Pringles etc. that were mockingly called "The Bonnie Jumper Squad". One of their number was a lad called Lambsy, who lived around the corner from me, and he had a girlfriend from Liverpool. He took note of what was happening in Merseyside and soon put our dress sense right. The "Bonnie Jumper Squad" would soon morph into the more serious Newcastle Mainline Express (NME). By '83/'84, Newcastle had more than caught up with the rest of the country and would go on to be one of the most clued-up mobs in the country.

Anyone who disputes that wasn't there, as the saying goes.

In 1987, I started following England and went to a couple of lively games at Hampden and was in Germany for the Euros in '88. Around this time, I also moved to London for work but would still follow Newcastle when they visited the south east. However, in the late 80s, it's safe to say that football was on the wane as acid house and raves seemed to be the order of the day. For London games, I used to meet my mates coming off the train at King's Cross. One of these games was in October 1988 just after the Euros: West Ham away. We had arranged to meet up with some of the West Ham England lads. West Ham won 2-0, but I didn't go to the match, and instead ended up drinking around all the Hammer haunts, including The Boleyn, The Queens, The Prince and a little mock wine bar that was tucked into the corner of the market, called JRs. Although there isn't much love lost between West Ham and Newcastle, a kind of begrudged respect emerged at that time. Let's just say members of both fraternities shared business interests related to the acid house scene. I have to say my two mates and I were treated well and ended up going on a bit of a mission to Bethnal Green, related to doormen and Chelsea.

My musical tastes were changing, I couldn't really get into the house music lark and so like many others I got into bands like the Happy Mondays and The Farm. I remember a great Farm gig at Newcastle Mayfair circa 1990. It was the first concert that my future wife and I went to together and little did I know that the gig would end up in forming some good friendships many years later. Through the early 90s, football was still part of my life but took a bit of a back seat as I got married in '92 and we had our first child in '94. Nevertheless, all the young family distractions didn't stop me enjoying the Keegan and Robson managerial years with a few unforgettable trips to Europe following Newcastle.

Since 2003, I've resided in Murcia, Spain. I have fallen out of love with the modern game, especially the shenanigans of Newcastle United and what it has become. However, I do still follow the results and take an interest in some aspects of Spanish football. In fact, a few years ago I wrote a book about the lower tiers of Spanish football and the sub-culture that has built up around it. I often return to the UK and still meet up with some of the old Newcastle faces. I also like to see them when they come over to Spain, usually Benidorm. Additionally, I have made it a Christmas tradition to go back to London and see the Cockney

Rejects in Islington. I am happy to say I've made some good acquaintances with a number of the West Ham lads, who also attend that annual gig.

Chris W – Leeds

"For those involved, no explanation is needed. For those not, no explanation is possible."

I was born exactly a month after England won the World Cup in 1966, seven minutes after my identical twin brother, "our kid" Stephen, in Leeds, part of Yorkshire in England. The true centre of the world!

Mum worked part time as a florist. Dad was a wheelwright, then a driver and later a clippie, to name but a few. He was even a trainee electrician until he realised he was colour blind, silly sod! They bought a back-to-back terrace house in the East End Park area of Leeds. Coal fire, tin bath. Poor, proud and happy. Me and "our kid" started at the local primary school at the age of four years and four months.

It was around this time that Mum and Dad started to take us down to Elland Road to watch the famous Leeds United. Bremner, Giles... *that* Leeds United. First, we'd go to Edmond House Social Club, in East End Park, then drive to the White Hart in Beeston, have a drink of pop and packet of crisps in both, before walking down the hill to "church". Mum loved football as much as the rest of us, even though most of her side of the family were, and still are, Rugby League fans ahead of football. To be honest, I don't remember much about any specific games until Jack Charlton's testimonial game, May 7th 1973, against Celtic.

Of course, I remember the television showing the Centenary Cup final in 1972, 6th May, Mum's birthday. Leeds against Arsenal; probably the best two teams around at the time. "Clarke, one nil!" King Billy, up the steps to collect the FA Cup from Her Majesty, or "our Lizzy" as we called her in the family. Mick Jones, in pure agony, helped up the steps by that giant of a man, Norman Hunter to collect his medal. Wow, just wow. We are Leeds and we do it our way and our way alone.

Our little back-to-back house was compulsory purchased for slum clearance by Leeds City Council not long after I started school. It had been paid for within four years, yet they gave our parents less than it was worth. To sweeten the loss, they offered them a council house in North Leeds. Grandma, Mum's mother, had moved there from Hunslet, South Leeds when they were built in the early 1950s. This was, and still is, the "posh end" of Leeds. Life was good. Good schools, nice house, garden etc. A little brother soon arrived on the scene, our Andy. He followed in our footsteps football-wise and is a well-known and respected lad in his own right.

Mum stopped going to matches once she started working all the hours God sent, so Dad's cousin Gary came. He was in his twenties, so was dressed like the younger fans. A great bloke, great fun. As me and "our kid" got older, we started to stand a little bit further and further away from Dad and Gary, and eventually we were allowed to go to a different part of the ground. The famous "Boys' Pen" in the corner of the Elland Road Kop. By now, we were being mesmerised by Tony Currie banana shots and the best Leeds home and away kits ever worn, with the best club badge.

A rite of passage at Elland Road was to climb into the Kop from the Boys' Pen and get in amongst the "blokes". Large, standing terraces were absolutely packed everywhere back then. Swaying, heaving masses of humanity. As a twelve- to thirteen-year-old, it was f***ing awesome!

Soon, me and "our kid" started to go to some games on our own. This freedom meant we were able to watch the mayhem, without being dragged away. We could shout and scream, like everyone else, at the poor sods visiting to watch their team. Violence was common. It was just how it was. Being from a nice area, we weren't as used to it as maybe some of the lads from rougher parts, but we had family history in Hunslet and Seacroft, tough places, so I guess it's kind of built in!

One mid-week, we played Scum (Manchester United) at home. We could get the bus outside the ground, all the way across Leeds to the end of our street, but we used to walk back to the town centre with the hordes. After this game, at Holbeck Moor, Leeds fans waited behind hedges, cars, whatever, for the Scum escort to get halfway across the moor and then all hell broke loose. They were attacked from everywhere. It made the papers. We were buzzing on a rush of adrenaline.

We started going to away games with a few mates from school. Football specials to places like Liverpool, great days out. Being the turn of the 1980s, it was a quick learning curve about how to survive in places that didn't like you very much at all. Eventually, we dumped the special trains and, with new mates made at home and away games, started travelling on the service trains.

In 1981, Leeds won at Old Trafford in a night match. Bryan Flynn scored ten minutes from the end.

87

Unsurprisingly, violence flared as Leeds fans climbed up to punch rivals in the seats above us. The police charged in to where we were and me and "our kid" were grabbed. Being teenagers, we were easy targets. We were frogmarched into the turnstiles. I was put in the bit where the bloke sits and "our kid" in the walkthrough part. We were mercilessly beaten by the Old Bill before being thrown out, as thousands were leaving, none too happy. Again, mayhem.

By the time the train pulled into Leeds station, my face and body were black and blue and my right eye swollen and completely closed. Mum, bless her, was waiting to collect us, with "our Andy" in the car. Needless to say, she was far from impressed. Andy thought it was great! We eventually got a formal apology from Greater Manchester Police, after Mum marched us down to Millgarth nick in Leeds to make a complaint. We decided all is fair in love and war and if that was the way it was, then so be it. Lesson learnt.

In 1982, my beloved team were relegated. The anti-hooligan fence at the Hawthorns was ripped down as a final farewell to the top division. It may seem a bit odd but the next ten years in Division 2, as it was known then, were brilliant. Shite football, shite grounds but bloody good fun. We went on adventures all over the

UK, following Leeds. We went to Blackpool for bank holiday weekends, a couple of hundred at a time; often straight to an away game on the Monday. Main Road was one. Everyone was carrying a HEAD bag, not hard to spot for the locals. Days out at places as far apart as Plymouth and Carlisle were fun and violent, madness and pure joy. We were having the time of our lives. It was a great time for music too. Leeds was still run down and dirty and there were nowhere near as many pubs or bars as these days, but we loved it.

If you were one of us, you were somebody. From the older lot, Ricky B, Eddie C, Alan P, Bob S, Slaney etc. to the likes of Griff, Sean R, Skizz, China, Myles and Kieran, and even the younger ones like Little Terry, we could do anything. The world was our oyster.

The football was still shite but improving. We got to an FA Cup semi-final and our first ever play off final were highlights, even though we lost both. There was the "Flying Leeds Fan" away at Oxford (it's on YouTube, worth a watch), the riots at Birmingham, Odsal and Bournemouth, mixed in with long weekends in Great Yarmouth for Norwich away – mud wrestlers, fancy dress, sleeping in vans; twenty-four-hour cafes at King's Cross... plenty of court appearances and some heavy sentences.

I was seventeen when Derby played at Elland Road and I got arrested before the game when a fight broke out outside the ground. I was still seventeen when it got to court. I was eighteen by the time I was released. "Our kid" was not happy that our eighteenth birthday party was delayed by two weeks. Mum was not happy when the service crew lads we invited started fighting with local lads trying to gate-crash. What are you gonna do?

I've had convictions since and a few close shaves. Growing up this way made me stronger, tougher and opened my eyes to things I had no knowledge of. I found out I could keep a clear head when trouble was brewing, so later spent years working the doors in Leeds. I enjoyed travelling about, so eventually I went to live and work abroad in Lanzarote. I spent a couple of years playing football in the pyramid, to see what level I could reach. I got a driving job due to my geographical knowledge of the UK, born from following Leeds on away days. I have mates that I met going to Leeds when we were about fifteen, who I still see at most matches to this day. Friendships forged in battle but also in fun. Bonds that can never be broken. I've been flown to Stockholm to appear in a kit launch video for Nike, through mates who support AIK Stockholm and come to watch Leeds. I have friends in Norway and Northern Ireland and the USA, all because of Leeds United. I've been locked up, fined, stabbed, hit over the head with an iron bar, beaten black and blue, all because of Leeds United.

My friends, Chris Loftus and Kevin Speight, died following our team. They are never forgotten. I played football for years with Chris and his brothers and we are still mates. I know everyone who was there. All the faces on the news. I see their pain on the anniversary. No one should go to a match and never come home. No one ever.

I wore Fila and Tacchini, Armani and Gee2, Lois and Levi's, 3 Stripes and Wallabies. Stone Island and Barbour. I could go on all night about the clothes, the fashion, the culture.

Leeds United has shaped me as a person, shaped my life in every way. I've lost relationships from going to football, putting Leeds first. I've been a s**t dad, honestly. Always tried my best but it just never worked out as it should. Lots of making right still to be done. I went to see my daughter recently and we went for a drink and some food. Her mum Debi and I get on really well. Much better, to her credit, than I deserve. She said something that made me think but also made me smile... "Your problem is, your one and only true love is Leeds United."

She was right. Of course, I love my kids, my family and friends in various ways. My exes too. They all got me to where I am today. Leeds, I have to admit, has been the one constant, undying love. I loved living in Lanzarote, but the thing I missed more than anything, was Leeds United. Match days with the lads. Beers, stories, laughs.

Where am I today? Back in Leeds. I now have an issue with my health that affects my optical nerves. In short, I am slowly going blind. It will never improve but could stabilise. I can't see well enough to drive or work. My overall vision allows me to function pretty well but a large part is simply blurred. For this reason, I haven't been to a game, home or away, for a while now. Well, pre-COVID, as I can't see the ball. Deciding not to go has killed me; but sadly, not as much as going to my church, Elland Road, and being unable to enjoy it as I used to. Needless to say, my football mates are relentless in their piss-taking. I don't know how I would manage without them. I think you get the impression I am trying to make. The point? Football is life and life is football. Why? Why not?

Paul – Fulham

Ironically the day that Jason contacted me to write a piece for his book, I had managed to score myself a pair of Adidas "Stan Smiths" for less than twenty-five pounds. I usually wear Gazelles or Sambas but couldn't resist buying them for the sale price and I think they are a great looking pair of trainers. But more on my fashion tastes later.

So how did I come to get into football? My dad was born right at the start of the second World War and was brought up in the Lewis Trust buildings, Fulham Broadway, which was a stone's throw from Stamford Bridge. He was an only child for the first nine years of his life until my two uncles came along in 1948 and 1949 respectively. Sometime in the late 1940s/early 1950s, my great uncle took him to see Fulham play at Craven Cottage. He can't remember the game but told me he had no interest in football then, so spent the whole match playing around in the enclosure now known as the Johnny Haynes stand.

In September 1953, a friend of his who was a mad Chelsea fan took him to Stamford Bridge and for the first time, he was captivated by the whole experience of going to a football game. The following Saturday, Fulham were playing at home against Nottingham Forest, so my dad decided to go along and saw Fulham win 3-1. A certain Bobby Robson scored one of the Fulham goals in front of a crowd of just over 24,000. My dad took one look at the ground and decided that this was the team he was going to support. It was on this day my football supporting destiny was decided. If on the other hand, he had decided that Stamford Bridge and the more fashionable and ultimately more successful Chelsea was the place for him, my football supporting life would have been very different to what I've experienced.

I was born in South London in September 1965 and my dad first took me to see Fulham play on Boxing Day 1972; a 1-0 win over Millwall. I was seven years old at the time so I can't remember too much about the match but I remember enough to become hooked on the beautiful game. I didn't see another match until August of 1975 as my dad worked a lot of Saturdays, but from that day, football was all I really ever thought about. Up until I started going to games on my own in about 1981, we would see anywhere between five to ten home games a season.

I can remember the first time I ever saw or became aware of fashion on the terraces. It was a game against West Ham at Craven Cottage in November 1978. A school friend of mine was a Hammers fan. His dad took both of us and we stood on the Putney terrace which is the away end at Craven Cottage. I remember there were skinheads everywhere and, being thirteen at the time, I was fascinated by their Doc Marten boots, Sta Prest trousers and Harrington jackets more than anything else. Luckily, the game ended 0-0 so I didn't have to run the risk of getting my head kicked in if Fulham scored.

My parents moved us out of London to Crawley, Sussex in 1969. I had a happy working, middle-class childhood. We lived in a nice house and went to a decent school. Unfortunately, my parents separated in 1978, but my dad continued to take me to Fulham when my sister and I stayed with him at weekends. In 1981, I was allowed to go to my first game on my own. By this time, Fulham had been relegated to the old Division 3, and I went to see Fulham play at home to Chester.

We won 2–0. The date was 26th September – exactly the same date as when my dad first went to Craven Cottage twenty-eight years earlier. It also turned out to be a successful season for Fulham as we won promotion back to Division 2.

It was around the start of the 1982/83 season that I started to notice the casual scene at football matches. I was at Crawley railway station with my best mate at the time, Simon Franklin, another Fulham devotee. We were going up to a game in London and I noticed a bloke of about nineteen or twenty years old with a mullet haircut, Pringle jumper, Lyle & Scott roll neck, faded jeans and a pair of Adidas Borg Elites and I thought how bloody good he looked. I then started noticing the casual fashion every game I went to and wanted a piece of it. Of course, like any young man of seventeen, earning twenty-five pounds a week on a youth training scheme and buying expensive sportswear was out of my reach. And I was too chicken to nick it from the shops. So, I persuaded my parents to give me some money. I kitted myself out with a Patrick burgundy cagoule, a pair of faded Levi's and a pair of Nike Blue Flash trainers. I thought I looked the dog's bollocks.

In 1978, I had started at Thomas Bennett Comprehensive School in Crawley. At one time, it was in the Guinness Book of Records for having the most pupils of any school in Britain. It was also the school that ex-Chelsea and Plymouth midfielder Brian Bason had attended when he was picked to play for England schoolboys. It was more of a rugby playing school, and all three of our P.E. teachers were Welsh and really didn't like football. Most of my mates hated rugby and were as mad about football as me. It was regarded as the roughest school in Crawley but there were plenty of Fred Perry polo shirts, Harrington jackets etc. being worn as can be seen in the different class photos people post on Facebook these days.

For me, going to football in the early to mid-80s wasn't about the fighting, but certainly was about the clothes we wore and the whole match day experience of the time. Even though I had been going to football for ten years by 1982, I had only ever seen Fulham play away once. But by the start of the 1982/3 season, I was seventeen, and now with a bit of cash in my pocket, I could start following Fulham up and down the country. Yet the first away game I ever attended on my own was Crystal Palace – one of the closest grounds to where I lived in Crawley at the time. I loved it and wanted more, and ended up seeing nine away games that season. I encountered my first taste of football violence and just how badly the police treated football fans at the time, especially those of us from London and the south.

Simon and I went up to Leicester in December 1982. There were only about 250 of us but were met off the train by the police and escorted to Filbert Street. It was the first time I had experienced anything like it, but the buzz was great. It was that feeling of all being together in enemy territory. As I mentioned, getting involved in fighting at football never appealed to me. Probably because I was shit scared of getting a good kicking or worse, and then having to face the wrath of my parents. Fulham were unlike teams such as Millwall, Chelsea, West Ham, Portsmouth or even Cardiff and Birmingham. We never had or will have a violent following and so my exposure to football violence was somewhat limited (not that I really wanted it). Had my dad decided all those years ago to stick with Chelsea then things for me would have been decidedly different. That's not to say Fulham didn't have a few faces that could look after themselves and had a bit of a crew known as The Thames Bank Travellers. They were not in the class of the ICF, the Chelsea Head-Hunters, Leeds Service Crew or Portsmouth's 6.57 Crew, but certainly had their moments.

Going to away games in the early 80s was a dangerous business, especially up north. One such incident, and the first time I had ever found myself in the middle of a scuffle, was at Oldham in January 1983. It was an FA Cup third round tie which we had just won 2-0, and as we came out of the ground, were set upon by Oldham fans. The next thing I knew I was on the ground with three or four blokes laying into me. Now as I said, I was never into violence, but on the other hand, if someone was going to have a go at me, I wasn't just going to sit there and take it. I started kicking back and the next thing I knew I was back up on my feet, a bit shaken but managing to get out alive, and back on the train safely to London. I wouldn't say I got the thrill many casuals have said they've experienced from having a good ruck at football, but it wasn't anywhere as bad as I thought it would be. To be fair, back then it was mostly handbags, with fans gesturing to each other to come and have a go; the more serious violence came much later as portrayed in films like *Green Street* and *The Football Factory*, at least that's how I remember it.

To counter my last point, it was on the last day of the 1982/3 season that I witnessed hooliganism at its worst. On that day, Fulham played away against Derby, and were still in with a chance of promotion to the old first division. Also, Millwall were playing away at Chesterfield and West Ham were playing away at Coventry. We had decided not to go on the official chartered supporters train, and so were sitting waiting on an Intercity 125 at St. Pancras station, surrounded by some of Millwall's finest. All of a sudden, a fair few of them spotted some West Ham fans outside, clambered off the train and had a right tear up with the Hammers.

Fulham's game at Derby later that day has been well documented but is still worth recalling. In a nutshell, Fulham were in fourth position in the old Division 2 at the start of play that day, and needed to better Leicester City's result to get promoted to the top division. Derby, on the other hand, had to win to be certain of not being relegated. Now anyone who ever went to The Baseball Ground as an away supporter will know it wasn't the nicest place to visit; it was in every sense of the word an old school ground nestled in amongst terraced houses and industrial buildings. The walk from Derby Midland station wasn't the most pleasant either. We tried to keep our heads down and hoped that nobody would come up to us with that age old trick of asking if we had the time so they could hear our accents. Fulham ended up losing the game 1-0 and with it the dream of promotion was gone. But the result is not what the match is most remembered for. After Derby scored, their fans invaded the pitch and the rest of the game was played in the most intimidating atmosphere I have ever experienced as a Fulham fan. Derby supporters were allowed to stand virtually on the touchline for the last fifteen minutes of the game. At one point, a Fulham player, Robert Wison, was kicked by a Derby supporter. Where we were stood, on the terrace behind the goal, wasn't much better – we were pelted with coins and other objects and at one point even a pig's head is said to have been thrown, but I never saw that.

Portsmouth's Fratton Park was another great old school ground that I loved visiting. It is the only ground I have ever been ejected from. On New Year's Eve 1983, Fulham where winning 1-0 when the Pompey fans sang the famous Pompey Chimes which as most fans know goes, "Play up, Pompey. Pompey, play up," to which away fans would sing back, "Fuck off, Pompey Pompey, fuck off." Swearing at football, although not to everyone's liking, is almost part of the match day ritual and has been ever since a crowd first watched a game. It seemed on this particular day that the Hampshire constabulary were having none of it, and about five or six of us were grabbed by the police and marched out the ground. We were then told in no uncertain terms to "piss off back to London" but we had the last laugh as Fulham won 4-1.

Just over a year later on New Year's Day 1985, we again found ourselves travelling down to Portsmouth. We were 4-0 down at halftime, with a stinking hangover from the night before and the biting wind blowing in off the Solent. Some of us tried to leave but the police wouldn't let us, how's that for irony? But it was just as well, as Fulham fought back to draw 4-4. The police kept us in for a good half an hour after the final whistle, with the 6.57 Crew more than likely waiting for us outside. It was a bit hairy getting back to Fratton station.

I got married and then had my children in the early 90s. This, along with Fulham's demise and relegation to the old Division 3, and eventually Division 4 between 1986-1996, meant away trips were curtailed a little, but I still continued to go to most home games. By this time, the casual scene wasn't as strong as it once was, and football violence for a while certainly wasn't as bad as it was. So, going to away games certainly didn't feel like you were taking your life into your own hands anymore. Although both were still bubbling under the service.

Simon and I had lost touch so I usually went with a couple of different mates and my dad, sharing a couple of pints in the Spotted Horse pub in Putney High Street, or The Crabtree in Fulham. The only violence I have really encountered in recent years was after a game away to Birmingham City right at the start of the 1999/2000 season. We were pegged back to 2-2 from leading 2-0, with Stan Collymore playing for Fulham, getting dog's abuse for most of the game from the Brummie fans and we also had Geoff Horsfield sent off. We left the ground to get back to the coach. A policeman came aboard and told us to draw the curtains and keep our heads down. As we left St. Andrews, the coach was pelted with bricks. One came through the window and straight out the other side. The police didn't seem to want to stop it, maybe they hated southerners too.

Of course, the casual scene was really the only youth culture born out of football and fashion, rather than out of music. Punk was defined by groups like Sham 69 and the Sex Pistols. Teddy boys by the music of Bill Haley and Elvis Presley, and New Romantics by Duran Duran and Adam and The Ants. But there was never really one musical genre you could exclusively attach to casuals. My musical tastes varied but I was a great fan of groups like Madness and The Jam. Also 60s mod groups like The Kinks and Small Faces. I also wasn't averse to a bit of Blondie, Duran Duran, even Phil Collins or Michael Jackson.

As I grew older, my favourite choice of clothes on match day were my Adidas Gazelles, Farah jeans and Reebok sweatshirt with a Harrington jacket, or Fulham Adidas jacket if it was cold. I am now fifty-five, but still like to dress in decent brands. For me, these days, it's brands that were never totally associated with casuals. I am a big fan of Ben Sherman and Fred Perry but it has to be Adidas Gazelles or Sambas, two of the greatest trainers ever designed. I have also bought a few bits from online store like 80s Casual Classics including a royal blue Fila Settanta tracksuit top which was way out of my price range back in 1983. I also buy from one of my favourite stores Lambretta in Carnaby Street whenever I am back home in London. They say that there is a crossover between mods and casuals. I tend to agree.

Today, I live thousands of miles from where I spent a massive part of my life, residing in Perth, Australia. I still go to football though, to watch Perth Glory in the Australian A- League as well as staying up all hours of the night to watch Fulham games. Admittedly, it is not the same as watching football back home in England, but with a large expat population living here, the casual influence can be seen at Perth Glory games. Men of my age and younger wear Lacoste, Ben Sherman and Fila polo shirts with Adidas Gazelles. I have been known to see the odd Sergio Tacchini or Fila track top. I also have a son who is fourteen and is just starting to take an interest in fashion; he likes Gazelles and Ben Sherman just like me, and loves listening to me telling him about going to games in the 80s: the dilapidated grounds, (often) s**t football and crowd trouble. He also can't believe just how bad Fulham once were!

As I said earlier, for me, casuals were all about football and fashion. There were those that loved a good ruck with opposition, but as much as I would gesture at opposing fans, the violence never interested me. I never saw the point in trying to kick someone's head in because of the team they supported or the part of the country they came from. I suppose that was the beauty of the casual movement: it was just that little bit different. As one media commentator once said, you could never quite put your finger on what casuals were all about.

Johnny Griff – West Ham

The lure of football was simple for me. I lived a ten-minute walk from Upton Park. All my family were Hammers supporters. I started going to reserve games when I was about eight years old with school mates. If you came from here, your team played in claret and blue, end of story.

The first big match I remember clearly was, wait for it, against Doncaster Rovers, Division 2 in 1955. My uncle George was a season ticket holder, upper tier westside. His pal couldn't go, so he took me. Wow, I was amazed, sitting up in the sky, gob-smacked. The Hammers hooked me. We won 6-1. My hero Harry Hooper 3, Billy Dare 1, Tucker 1, and Andrews 1. I know because I still have the programme with terrible handwriting on it as I listed scorers. I never was a good scholar.

I continued going when the ticket was available with Uncle George. The Chicken Run was an old wooden structure and I loved getting at the back when everyone sang "Bubbles" or "Bye Bye Blackbird" with the name for the opposition team, for example Bye Bye Blackburn or Blackpool. Any team would do. The whole Chicken Run swayed – top steps to the right, next row down to the left, until the whole of the Chicken Run was swaying. I still don't know how it never collapsed. I used to have a man with a post horn standing next to the tunnel as the players emerged, playing the team onto the pitch with the Post Horn Gallop. I never stopped going and always lived for Saturdays.

When I left school, I went on some away days, but the biggest for me, maybe still, was the trip to Hillsborough for an FA Cup semi-final against Manchester United in 1964 with Law, Best, Charlton and co. Happy Hammers won 3-1: Ticker Boyce 2, Geoff Hurst 1. It was an ankle-deep mudded pitch. It rained all day from midday; it never stopped. There wasn't a roof on the stand and we looked like drowned rats. Being a fashion-conscious mod, I wore my brand-new chocolate suede three-quarter length jacket to show the Mancs how smart Cockney boys dress. It was completely ruined, but I did not care as we were in the Cup final.

We sang our heads off all the way home on the train and Eastenders being proper, had a whip round for the train driver and presented it to him when we arrived back in London. I count myself blessed I was at all FA Cup semi-final and final victories, and for all my friends I have acquired through following the Hammers; some outstanding memories of happy and sad days, home and away, when you could take booze on the train to away games and load up for the return trip. We hardly ever won away. We had a party on the train home from Leicester because we drew. I had wonderful days away with John and Mandy Dillane, Nick Mayer. With John D driving, we got home so fast nobody believed you went, true! I ended up in Chav's Corner Upton Park, everyone's proper, with fantastic humour, wonderful songs. I miss them and I miss Upton Park.

My whole life revolved around West Ham Football Club. I even got married on a Friday, so that I wouldn't miss the match on Saturday. I also miss meeting up before the game and after. We always met up afterwards, if we won, drew, or lost, to have a booze.

For me, it all ended the night we walked out of Upton Park for the last time. They took away our ground, but they can't take away our memories.

Thank you, Jason, for the invite to partake. Special mention for Georgie Boyle who would have loved to have been involved in your book.

Terry Cecil – Aveley/Arsenal/Man City

I grew up in Aveley, Thurrock on a council estate built by the London County Council to house the bombed-out people from mostly the East End of London. My parents were from Bethnal Green and Hackney and lived through the war, which included being bombed as civilians, and fighting in it with the Navy. By the time they were allocated a council house in Aveley, they already had a small family. My dad got a job at the Ford factory in Dagenham and it was a new life for them.

However, all of their family and friends were back in town and most weekends or spare days, we all piled into a van, went up town and slept over at my nan's flat while my parents socialised. This meant I had mates in both areas and as there was nothing much to do back in the 70s besides knocking on neighbours' front doors and running off. Football was all we had.

Whether it was the ball court on the Pembury Estate or the green in front of the bus stop in Aveley, I was always playing football, talking about football or involved in some sort of football related pastime, such as collecting stickers or Super Striker. Super Striker was a cheaper version of Subbuteo where you pushed the players' heads down to make him kick a small ball. Seriously, the kids nowadays with their fancy Nintendo Switches and goodness knows what else don't know they're born. When I went back into Hackney with the family, I would spend most of my time in the ball court with friends but there was a chance that my elder brother might give me the nod and I'd go with him up the Balls Pond Road to see Arsenal. Real football.

At Highbury, there was a schoolboy enclosure section which is where I would go in on my own, or duck under the turnstile and get into the legendary North Bank if my brother could suffer me. The North Bank was where all the "geezers" would be, which was really exciting for a spotty kid but useless for actually seeing any of the game. In the schoolboy enclosure, you could always see the match and if you were lucky, get close enough to the substitutes of the opposition warming up on the touch line and tell them to f**k off. You also had to keep an eye on the other kids, especially if you were on your own, as it was always a bit lively in there, no adults and all that. But the North Bank was where everyone wanted to be; some Herbert's used to try to get in over the fence between the enclosure and the North Bank terrace or run onto the pitch and then get in that way. I never did, just being in the ground was enough of a buzz for me: the atmosphere, the swirling crowd, the bad language – it was brilliant. "Yeah, f**k off, Perryman!"

Seeing these actual footballers on the pitch was thrilling. Most kids at school only saw them on *The Big Match* but here I would be, at Arsenal, looking for where the cameras might be, in case I could get my ugly boat on TV. This was as good as it got in the 70s for a nine-year-old.

Back in Thurrock, Aveley had a football club, nothing like Arsenal of course, but a proper ground nonetheless, with floodlights and a stand. My mates who I played football with were a mix of Arsenal and West Ham fans. I think one of my mates supported Manchester United because he wanted a beard like George Best. I used to try to kick him the most. At some point, one of us had the idea to bunk into an Aveley game at The Mill Field. There was a hole in the fence and one Saturday, we decided to sneak in. I don't know what I was expecting after the glorious scenery I had experienced at Highbury. It certainly wasn't anything like that. The ground was sparsely occupied by old men and the game going on was dull, really dull, and worse still, I didn't recognise any of the players. We watched about five minutes before we set up a pitch behind one of the goals and played ourselves. Playing in a real football arena (of sorts) felt better than playing in front of the bus stop and it soon became something we would do often.

Eventually, the novelty wore off, habits changed and the older lads started to get girlfriends. However, a few of us still went to Aveley and began to watch the football itself. We started to get the bug and even bought blue and white scarfs to be proper fans. We were now paying to get in, sometimes if we were boracic, we'd wait for halftime when it was free, but we started to feel a part of the club and the club part of us. There was a big difference between Arsenal and Aveley. At Arsenal, it was all very exciting and the older I got, the more mischief I'd get into, especially if I went up from Aveley on my own. Whether that was little skirmishes around the ground, sneaking beer in the Lord Nelson or walking up to Finsbury Park for pie and mash while bizarrely singing loud in the street at strangers walking the other way.

The journey on the oxo to and from the game, was like running the gauntlet between West Ham and Dagenham East on the district line. This was bandit country when West Ham were at home, anyone under the age of twenty-five was taking their life in their hands travelling on this bit of the railway after 4:45 p.m. Would they suss that we were Arsenal? We would have to make sure we hid any colours we wore and then leg it to the bus stop for the 103. Exciting.

Down at Mill Field, it was the other side of the coin. Crusty old blokes with flat caps and walking sticks, the odd opposition supporter done up like a Christmas tree and covered in badges. I thought to myself even back then, *We don't need any stinking badges and I don't want to look like that.*

We wouldn't be allowed in the clubhouse without an adult; the burger bar was more than my pocket money could spare but I could get home after the game in time to find out the football results. That was a big bonus back then. Sometimes if we went to an Arsenal game, we wouldn't know any of the other results of the day until we had got home hours later. Sometimes you wouldn't find out until you saw the Sunday papers the next day. Mind you, at the time, often we wouldn't know any of the other teams' scores in Aveley's league until years later. I'm still finding out about them now. For some reason, it wasn't important then.

By the age of sixteen, I had found The Jam, bought a Vespa 50 and was spending all my spare cash on going to the Bridge House in Canning Town to see bands. Football took a back seat for a while but my social contacts had expanded and one of them, Potter, turned out to be an Aveley fan too. All the time I was going to Aveley as a kid, he was there too. Potter used to go with his old man and although I don't remember ever seeing him there, it was a funny coincidence and another thing that bonded us.

Another addition to my group of chinas was Stearny, an obnoxious character who dressed like a casual, with highlights in his hair but, importantly, he owned a car. Over time, the three of us started to return to Mill Field to watch Aveley again. This time with access to the clubhouse and the bar!

This was now the late 80s and Paul Weller had moved on to the Style Council which enabled me more time to do things like watching Aveley home and away. Stearny, Potter and I were super keen. Stearny had this Mini Metro and a proper job, so he would drive to the games with either Potter or me in the back getting our arses out down the A13 or something equally as ridiculous like giving Stearny directions. Potter did this one time on a dreary Tuesday night for an away game with the Met Police, taking the address from the Isthmian League Year book that he subscribed to, the k**b. It was only when the clock turned 7:30 p.m. and we were in the middle of bleeding nowhere that we decided to check Potter's directions. We discovered that instead of the football ground address, Potter had been looking at the wrong paragraph and we were now outside the Met Police's club secretary's house, in the wrong county and zero chance of watching any football.

The problem with the three of us was that we never took anything seriously, even Aveley. The other two had grown up with similar experiences to me and understood the bizarre differences between the big leagues and where Aveley were. So, we just went to a pub and talked about how s**t we thought the Style Council were. This was when we decided to jump on the football fanzine craze that was sweeping the country, led by When Saturday Comes magazine. All of the big teams had glossy fanzines that you could buy at games outside the ground. They were often a critical view of their clubs by fans, mixed with ideas from the popular adult comic of the day, Viz. Stearny worked (sic) in a printers in Old Street, and with his skills on publishing (and Potter's and mine of talking bollocks), we managed to put together an eight-page booklet called, There's Only One Reggie Harris. We thought about a few names, "Aveley, Not *as* S**t as Tilbury" for example, but settled on naming the fanzine after a player who refused to tuck his shirt in his shorts and could juggle the ball on the back of his neck.

The fanzine was utter fantasy. We turned the players from being part-time footballers and day-time Ford workers, to God-like heroes of Aveley and the civilised world. We would do bizarre things like pick a player of the month and present him with a free voucher from a local barber that we would buy for them. Players never won the prize for their football ability but for drinking eight pints after a game, for doing a long side tackle regardless of getting either the ball or the man, or for telling one of the opposition substitutes to "f**k off!" We would start to do stranger and stranger things to have stuff to write about. We went to games in fancy dress (it was funny at the time, it bloody was). Once, we set up a full drum kit in the East Stand. There were added bonuses to these stunts; two of our subs warming up against Wembley with Barny Rubble and

Fred Flintstone heads on was quite a sight. The drum roll and cymbal crash when one of the lads had a shot on goal often got a laugh, especially by the goalkeeper when we missed (which was always quite a lot). Aveley were never that good but you wouldn't have thought it reading the fanzine.

We would often shout out ridiculous things from the scantily populated terraces like, "run in an arch", "put them to the sword" or to the referee, "protect our talented stars... and Dayo". The small band of Aveley supporters would gather around us and soon our fanzine was more popular than the club programme, gaining some notoriety in the fanzine world. We used to give it away for free and were chuffed with ourselves for that. Then we learnt that some charlatans from Dagenham FC were churning out a single A4 sheet, folding it in half and giving that out. Not wanting to be outdone, as When Saturday Comes said at the time, we came across an ingenious marketing strategy by sticking a new penny to each copy of Reggie so that we were paying people to take our fanzine. Our motto was: "Satisfaction guaranteed or *our* money back".

In reality, the three of us wrote for each other's benefit. We would cross lines, accuse referees (with no evidence) of being Freemasons, ridicule those in positions of power in the club and the league, all while writing about Aveley as though they were Barcelona. Everything was tongue in cheek, but not everyone got the joke and before we knew it, the fanzine was banned at games by the Isthmian League when they found out about it. It was the beginning of the end. Stearny found a bird and that was that. The fanzine days were over and things drifted apart for a bit. We still went to a fair number of games but other things, like family and work would often get in the way. I then found out that I could play football to a reasonable standard, and that Potter and Stearny couldn't match it, so I spent a lot of time doing that on Saturdays and our time together on the terraces decreased as we hit our late twenties.

To us, Aveley was an outlet, a place we would meet up, where we could entertain ourselves with silliness and contribute to the community spirit of the club. We wanted to win, we craved winning but if we lost, so be it. By the time we arrived home, we would have forgotten about it and gone about our week, unless it was Tilbury. It was a loyalty card we could pick up and put down. I was never that interested in the league position, as long as we won more than we lost, I was fine.

We had the odd Cup final or promotion push, losing 5–0 in a Cup final to Chelmsford was brutal.

I also remember Martyn Hayes, formerly of Arsenal, playing for a newly reformed Romford and scoring a few times against us in another trophyless final. What a git. We used to put on the occasional end of season do for the players and have some good banter with different characters that came through the club. It was a good social place but as time went on Mill Field became a tired arena for football. Attendances were falling. Sometimes I would entertain myself (in the absence of the players doing that for me) by counting the crowd, sometimes with two hands. Thurrock had five non-league teams, and while we might not have been the most glamorous money bags, Purfleet and Grays Athletic were where the good football was at and anyone that was any good for us would soon be off to them. I remember looking around the ground one wet, windy evening against some God awful team from who knows where, thinking, *This can't go on.*

As Thurrock expanded, housing estates sprung up on all the available land around the ground and there seemed to be an inevitability about what was going to happen. One of the new residents even made a complaint to the local council about noise and the floodlights being on during evening games which the council had to consider seriously. Never mind that,

Aveley FC had been there since 1927 and the nosy neighbour had been there two minutes. Out of the blue, the club announced a deal with a house builder to buy the ground, our home since I was little, and build a new state of the art (-ish) stadium, a stone's throw from Mill Field. The new ground had a 3G pitch, a large bar and a balcony! We always wanted a ground with a balcony. "Tilbury haven't got a ground with a balcony," we said. There was a lot of publicity about the new stadium, so when the time came for us to leave Mill Field and say goodbye to the memories we had there, we were just too excited about the prospects of the new ground to care much.

Unfortunately for the three of us, we are now in our poxy fifties and nearly dead. With the new ground came a new band of younger supporters who have taken the club to their hearts. The club has tapped into the community like never before and at the last game, there were nearly 400 supporters at a league game. Four hundred! Even with taking Potter's socks off, we could never have counted that many. There is a nice feel about the club; people are happy to stay behind after games and socialise. With social media, the new Reggie's, who call themselves Sons of Aveley, are in charge on the terraces and they do a great job supporting the team. They bang drums, have flags, sing songs and make a right racket. I was never one for singing at a non-league game but I guess it's different when there are more than just the three of you. Potter, Stearny and I are nobodies now. We are faces in a crowd, old farts telling stories that no one want to listen to. "Yeah, like when we camped on the centre spot at Mill Field with a two-man tent and a bottle of Jack Daniels after the last game of the season..."

Aveley are quite good these days, which is really annoying because we looked like getting promoted the last season, bloody didn't. I was p***ed off for months. These are new experiences for ex-Reggies, the threesome, in a fancy home, winning a lot, decent Guinness, burgers that don't taste like they have been made out of former players' carcasses and season tickets... we have season tickets now. This is football in the twenty-first century and man, how it has evolved. At this level, it is a wonderful glue that can bring people together, give them something to be part of with lots of youth teams representing the club. A place where youngsters will come and learn about teamwork, skills, camaraderie and how s**t Potter was at left back (surely that is part of the FA curriculum).

The professional game may still have the glamour, the fancy scenery and the famous names but the game has been stolen, even actual foreign states are buying clubs for PR purposes and it's getting more and more difficult to get close enough to tell the opposition subs to "f**k off!" Not that that's to be encouraged, but you know what I mean, like everything else, it's all changed. Some things these days have changed for the better (Paul Weller, Stearny's dress sense, my new Vespa scooter) but I can't help thinking that most of it has not. That's the beauty of getting older and I guess the beauty of the game. Football, from top to bottom. As The Jam said with their last live album before they signed off in 1982, "Dig the new breed!"

Alan Bates – Arsenal

I was born in a two-up, two-down with an outside khazi in the Archway, north London in the mid-60s. Quite a rough area to grow up in, not that you know that as a kid. When they knocked down the house to build a massive estate, we moved down to a big old red brick estate on Brecknock Road. This is the place where I first saw and encountered violence. Lots of violence. Housing estate fights were massive in the 1970s and we would watch from the balconies. My mum was from a family of eleven, so I had seen uncles and cousins having a punch-up at the social club, but never thought anything of it.

My first encounter of physical violence was when a kid from another estate had his football nicked and was punched by a blond kid from my flats. Unluckily for me, I was an eight-year-old blond kid kicking a ball around when a group of older kids surrounded me. I had never seen these boys before and I was terrified.

The older brother of the kid who was crying was telling him to bash me up to prove that he wasn't scared. He was crying and poking me in the chest, and from memory I wasn't crying but, frozen stiff, rigid with fear.

At this stage, my older sister who was fully grown at four feet ten inches tall, was watching from the balcony. God put this girl in a small package in order to protect society from her fearless attitude. She has the heart of a lion. She came down when all this commotion and baying for a fight was going on and whispered to me, "If you don't bash him up, I will fucking bash you up." Needless to say, I was more scared of my sister than any group of boys. I do not need to write any more about that episode.

When I was nine, the flats at the Archway were completed and we moved back to the estate, into this brand spanking new gaff with three bedrooms and two toilets. *Two* toilets. Wow, paradise. On my first day in primary school, I met George L, Stuart C and Robert P. I'll never forget these three. Stuart and Robert held my arms while George repeatedly kicked me in the shins with his Doc Martens boots, asking, "Does this hurt? Did that hurt?" "No, no, no," was my response. Years later, I realised that the better option would have been to say yes and cry, but I couldn't on that particular day. I did, in later years, get both Robert and Stuart back. It must have affected me because it was forty-six years ago and I still remember their names as if it was yesterday.

On the estate, there was a kid called Andy B, whose dad Charlie was a Chelsea fan and they both went every other Saturday and stood in the Shed to the right-hand side near the floodlight. They started to take me with them and I would hear the Shed sing songs to the North Stand, watching scuffles with the Old Bill running around. We walked out of the forecourt one day and there was a battle going on outside: skinheads everywhere, police horses, noise and chaos everywhere around. I must have been ten years old and not at any stage was I scared. I was so excited.

This started a weird fascination with football and gangs. I went to a couple of Spurs games with kids off the estate; didn't like anything about it there. I walked along with an older kid after a game and three or four young Spurs boys came over and said, "Who you support?" The older boy with me, pushed me and said, "Run!" which I did. He stayed and they attacked him.

I went to the QPR versus Spurs FA Cup final replay and watched an almighty tear up under the ramp at Wembley. This was more and more becoming such an adrenaline rush. In those days in London, you could buy a red bus rover, a ticket that got you all around London, all day. We ended up in Greenwich, South London – now this was an adventure. When we were at the Cutty Sark, these older boys were talking about Charlton playing West Ham and it was only up the road. Guess where we ended up. I witnessed turnstiles being knocked over, a fire in the Charlton end, and if my mind is not playing tricks on me, I am sure that there was a geezer in a gorilla outfit jumping around the flames. This was beyond belief. The next thing I saw was a group of the meanest looking men imaginable, and a strong-looking, cross-eyed man with them. I heard Millwall, and then boom.

The journey home to north London was electric. We went through New Cross and as the rattler pulled up, a West Ham fan shouted to the whole carriage, "No one fucking runs." I got home that night to find out that my parents had called the police as I was six hours late. You didn't get grounded in those days. Dad dealt with it differently.

There was a kid on our estate from Ireland called Kieran G who supported Leeds and he knew Cockney Whites – that's what they called themselves. We met them at Liverpool Street and they met up with the northern lot, all jean jackets and DM boots, long hair and scruffy. I sat on the train listening to stories, banter and they even had a bird with them called Sally who liked a row.

I was one of those kids who had loads of cousins, went to a school in a different borough to the one I lived in. Had grown up on a different estate in another part of Islington until I was nine, so I knew kids from Somers Town, Euston, Holborn, Holloway, the Cally and so on. It wasn't long before we started hovering around Euston, watching what was going on every Saturday, until the day that three of us got caught by some Cockney Reds, older blokes, twenty-ish. We were probably thirteen or fourteen. This geezer slapped me around the face every time he asked us a question, "Who are ya? Where are you from?" Each time slap, slap. "We are f***ing Cockney Reds, you little mugs." That was a trick because they wanted a reaction. They were Liverpool Cockney Reds. As luck would have it that night, from the escalators a f***ing big mob could be heard and these lads ran off sharpish... not without one last slap around the face for me. I felt like Balotelli. *Why me?* Can you believe that we were saved by a group of drunk Welsh rugby fans? They had no idea how much we loved them that night and no idea what had just happened to us.

By now, I was fully fledged at this football malarkey. I was working at my dad's work on Saturday mornings and every school holiday to get enough dough for away days, my trainers and clothes. The clobber in the early days became another obsession. There were a few shops where you could get your Sergios and Filas. There was one called Nick Naks down in Soho. Now this was a gaff that you had to be very careful with, because the Cockney mobs were all over it and then the northerners got on it too so you could have got taxed and bashed at any given moment.

A gaff opened in Camden Road and the bloke who owned it would let you pay for clobber weekly until it was yours and bam. We thought we looked the bollocks. Loved it there and there wasn't much chance of getting taxed on that manor. Sometimes we had to venture to Stag Sports on Tottenham High Road; now that was a whole new adventure. We soon realised that the northerners and other London mobs were proper on the clobber. I won't go down the route of a bickering match with whether Scousers and Mancs started the casual thing. All I will say is that if, and in my mind it's a big *if*, they started it, it wasn't long before they were begging us on the other side of fences to tell them where we got our trackies and trainers.

As we started early on, realising that we were Arsenal, and not only did we want to be the best mob, we had to be the best dressed firm in the country. I could never wear Lyle & Scott because West Ham wore it. I honestly got my first bit of Lyle & Scott at the age of fifty-three, and it was only because they do big sizes, but I just would not wear it because of West Ham. We started wearing Jaeger, Cerrutti and Valentino. I had a Ball jumper that had a bright orange zip. Little did I know that when you are dressed like a flash c**t and stand out a bit at football, the enemy remembers your face. I will soon come back to Valentino.

In 80s London, there were disco pubs everywhere. Islington joins onto Hackney, Camden and Haringey. So, we were basically surrounded by West Ham and Spurs. It was f***ing heaven. No mobile phones. Going down to Hackney knowing that a few ICF were there and couldn't do a thing because they would get smashed. Next week, you wouldn't go as you'd heard that they had a firm waiting for you. We were in the Dun Cow on the Old Kent Road in South London, the same thing happened, couple of slaps got dished out and a few bouncers got clumped. Great nights. We'd go up to Wheatley's at Wood Green and as soon as we got in there, within minutes we were sussed by Spurs and a brawl started that just got out of hand. I ran up towards the bus garage in my fake crocodile skinned shoes with leather soles, slipping everywhere, laughing my head off.

We once got in a scuffle outside a trainer shop on Westbourne Grove in West London. Goodness knows how, we'd heard that this gaff was selling Diodora Ed Moses. Off we went, tubes and buses, one of us had some amyl nitrate and we were on the back of the bus messing about and having a laugh. We got to the shop and there were a few bods milling around. You know how it starts. "All right! Where are you boys from?" "Archway." "Arch where, you fucking mug?" Bang. We never got our trainers that day.

I am probably boring the life out of you now and I have tried to not mention what went on so much at the games and our midnight walks around the Euston and the like. I could write for hours and hours about battles on and off the terraces. Mickey Droy`s testimonial in '84 and the unknown herd taking it to Chelsea on their own forecourt. West Ham at Zero 6 nightclub in Southend. Millwall in Highbury Fields, Millwall at The Blind Beggar in Whitechapel. River boat eighteenth birthday parties on the Thames and walking up to Busby at two in the morning because you heard that QPR and Chelsea were in there.

Valentino. I had this Valentino top, white with a purple collar, a yellow patch on one elbow, a red patch on the other and a cracking V crest right where your heart is. It was a nice sunny day and we were playing Liverpool. We sat in with them and as the teams were coming out, we sang *our* song, "She Wore a Yellow Ribbon" and it all went off. Benetton shirts everywhere. You could tell we were Arsenal because we already had the green ones. No, not me, silly bollocks wore the stand out Valentino to show the northerners how to dress. The brawl went for a while and great fun was had by all. The Walrus (our mad copper) and his little firm got us back to the other side of the fencing. We started chatting with their lot and agreed to leave a bit earlier. The streets were where it was going to be. We finally caught up with them on the top of Blackstock Road and we went backwards and forwards a few times, neither getting a real advantage until one last push from us and they were off on their toes, virtually disappearing into thin air.

By now, we were at Highbury Corner and this copper grabbed my face and as he said "Where do you live?", he banged my head on the door of the Barclays bank outside Highbury and Islington station. I told him the Archway. He said, "I've seen you in the thick of it three times today. Now do yourself a favour and get on that bus and f**k off home, otherwise I will nick ya." I decided to get on the bus with a few pals. We got to the Archway and for those of you that don't know it, it's the top of Holloway Road, the A1 North. We walked past Kentucky and there were a few recognisable faces in there. I pointed out the Scousers we had it with earlier on to Clive S (RIP). No questions asked, we were in the Kentucky's knocking the f**k out of everyone. Little did we know that they were not only in the Kentucky, but the chippy and the Wimpey.

We bit off way more than we could chew, and knowing the manor, made a tactical retreat.

I went home and showered. Then, at roughly eight in the evening that Saturday, I was standing on the corner waiting for a pal and he saw me from a distance and screamed, "Al, run!" I wondered what the f**k he was on about and then realised that a mini bus had pulled up beside me and they were pouring out of it to get to me. I ran onto the estate to my sister's place.

She was at my mum and dad's caravan and there I was in my highly noticeable, give it large, Valentino top on, smart as f**k. Surrounded by Scousers. I was beaten and trampled on so badly. The last words I heard were, "You're dead now, Cockney," as I fell unconscious, and I wet myself. The doctors told me that luckily I passed out and that would have stopped them kicking me to death. That wasn't enough though. One of them came back and cut my legs with a Stanley. I can never remember if I had forty-four or forty-eight stitches, but nonetheless I was in a bad way. My brain swelled and my left-hand side looked like a giant purple love bite. All because of that f**king Valentino top and Arsenal being the best dressed.

Once a casual always a casual.

Over the years, all the laughs that we've had together. That's why I go to West Ham.

Bonzo – West Ham

I grew up in Norwich about one hundred miles from London. My dad was a huge influence on me as a young boy. He was by profession a footballer, and as a young boy the house was always full of his mates (who also played). I can vividly remember Barry Butler playing with me as a six-year-old. He left the house and got killed going home, and has since been celebrated by giving his name to the Norwich player of the year trophy. My dad was a trainer at Norwich, so the house had several visits from their players. I can recall my dad taking my sister and I to the cinema to watch the World Cup final in colour as it was in black and white on the television. That was the start of my love affair with West Ham United.

I was Geoff Hurst mad. A few years later, my dad arranged for him to open a local sports shop. I was in heaven. As I got older, I started going to Norwich games as most kids did. I got involved with football hooligans and got nicked at Portsmouth in 1975 when I was fourteen. I went to loads of games, but always had my West Ham badge on. Things were changing on the fashion front. I had short hair and wore tonic trousers and Slazenger jumpers.

Moving on, after a few visits, it was August 1979 and I stayed in Wallasey on the Wirral and went to Wrexham away. We lost 1-0 but I was hooked and took a mate to Chelsea at home in the mid-week. They scored and he asked "Where are the Chelsea then?" There weren't any there.

(It's worth adding at this point that Bonzo is, and will be forever, a terrace legend. A right proper man, well respected and loved all over the country. A massive influence on myself and countless others. A friend and brother till the end. This man has your back!)

Riaz Khan – Leicester

As a kid, I never fitted in. Whether it was at school or outside of it. Born and bred in Leicester in the mid-60s, a Pathan, who are mainly from the north west frontier region of Pakistan and parts of Afghanistan. Leicester is a multicultural city and most of us live side by side, but that wasn't the case previously as there were a lot of racist attacks against the Asians and the Afro Caribbeans. Leicester in the 70s had the headquarters of the National Front, a right-wing political party who wanted to eject all ethnic minorities from the United Kingdom. In 1972, Idi Amin threw out all the Asians from Uganda. Uganda was part of the Commonwealth and 60,000 came to the UK. 20,000 settled in Leicester and this had an impact on ethnic minorities both positive and negative.

Thatcher became the prime minister in 1979 and she had an anti-immigrant stance. Her speech about "immigrants swamping the country" won her the election. So, it was a constant battle with some of the indigenous population who also held these political beliefs. You can imagine what it was like at school. It wasn't any different. A lot of the kids were harbouring these views because their parents did, so it wasn't really their fault. There were only a handful of ethnic minorities in school. Out of 1500 kids, there were around ten of us in total. It was difficult to fit in being Asian in a school with the majority being white with racist tendencies. To fit in, you had to follow a subculture of some sort, to be part of something.

The only culture available to me then was the Asian one and for some reason, it didn't appeal to me. I could not get into the music, the clothes (although I had no choice but to dress similarly) and the whole cultural package. Around the same time, there were punks, rockers, skinheads, boot boys, teddy boys, mods and goths. That period of school, the young kids dressed either as teddy boys or rockabillies with the duck's arse hairdos and crepe shoes. Then that changed to either skinheads, mods or rockers. I could never afford any of the clothing and my dress sense was terrible! I was once fortunate to receive a burgundy skier's jumper, a Harrington jacket and a couple of Fred Perry T-shirts because my mum's friend worked in a hosiery factory where she had access to slight seconds. Apart from that, I was always envious of the kids and the way they dressed at school. Even the skinhead style looked cool. Lambswool jumpers (mainly red), Fred Perry T-shirts, tight cropped jeans with Clarks desert boots (not the Doc Martins). I thought it was a great look. I just had to look and admire some of the dress styles.

When the New Romantic look came about, I had to have the flick style haircut but did not have the bottle (or the money) to go full out with the frilly pirate style shirts, baggy trousers and pixie boots! Some of the lads, in our final year at school in '82, spoke about the terraces at Leicester and how flick heads in the pens went steaming in with fists peddling away at the away fans that had infiltrated the home pen. I was further intrigued when one of them mentioned there was an Asian lad with big arms and ginger streaks in his hair, who stood in the pens with his arms crossed. I thought to myself that this lad must be dead hard to stand in the midst of these racist hooligans (that was the belief in those early days, that hooligans were part of the National Front). I also recall reading in a newspaper, that one of the lads from school gave me, of the Leeds Service Crew. There was a black and white picture accompanying the article of around twenty lads with flicks and wearing the clobber. I just remember staring at this picture for long periods and wishing to look like they did.

I didn't get the best results when leaving school, so my father sent me to sixth form college where I encountered Asian and black gangs. The thing in Leicester in those days, blacks and Asians were together (also some Irish) because of the racism, so they had a common enemy. Gangs were formed up and down the country mainly for protection. I reckon these lads watched the film *Warriors* which ignited this gang movement in the UK. I became a part of a gang for the same reason, as I had to venture into town daily to go to college. Even though I was a member of this gang, I still felt I did not belong, something was missing, but I could not place my finger on it.

One day in the spring of 1983, I was in a shopping mall. I used to hang out there for no reason with this gang, strange habit that was. I was on the first floor looking down when a group of lads walked through, about ten of them. They were led by a black lad. Something about these boys really caught my eye. It was the way they were dressed. I was in awe. It reminded me of the picture of the Leeds Service Crew. The clothes worn were a mixture of tennis and golfing gear with

139

white trainers and deerstalker hats. I had seen this group before, the previous summer when a few of them steamed into an older bloke who was baiting them for a fight. But I wasn't interested in the clothing they wore at that time; it was just the fight that enthralled me. One of the Indian lads I was with pointed to the black lad and said, "That's Ayman Paris, leader of the Baby Squad." I had no clue who they were, but all of them dressed in a certain way, and had a shared confidence in the way they walked. You could tell they had a special bond unlike anything I had seen in other gangs.

The Rasta who led these lads wore a red anorak and I wanted the same one. I went into all the sports shops and I thought I had found the jacket he was wearing. I started wearing a blue Patrick cagoule not realising the Rasta wore a Fila cagoule! I had to break away from that Asian look of Kung Fu slippers and tight jeans. Slowly, I started changing my look. And my younger brother followed suit. There was a place near to where we lived that sold golfing gear, labels like Slazenger (yep, it was cool back then in the late 70s, very early 80s), Pringle and Lyle & Scott. Also, they sold a range of zipped high neck cycling-type short sleeved tops that were worn under the V-neck pullovers. We managed to "acquire" a couple of bits and bobs from there and also bought some just to give the owners a kind of false sense of security, if you know what I mean (nudge nudge, wink wink). I started wearing this clobber around my estate (Rushey Mead) in the summer of '83. Tight bleached jeans, mushroom perm, Puma G-Villas, cycling tops worn with a Pringle jumper. I didn't care if it was hot. I just wanted to look the bollocks – and I did! So did my younger brother.

My younger brother had acquired a red Fila BJ Settanta track top and I wore it more times than he did (not realising that it had probably gone out of fashion by then). I remember walking through town late in the summer of '83, wearing that Fila BJ, a white Lyle & Scott roll neck, bleached jeans and Puma G-Villas (yes, I was hot) where there were members of the Baby Squad sat on and around a bench near the Clock Tower (which is in the middle of the city centre). I heard one of them say, "Who the f**k is that?" I turned and they were all looking at me. I was boosted. After a little while, I walked past them again, just to receive more attention and adoration (well, I thought it was that) but this time they looked at me, and it didn't look friendly. I caught the bus home as quickly as possible. That evening, I was thinking about those lads and wished that I had approached them to talk about the clothes they were wearing.

For the next few days, I was in the shopping mall again just hanging around when I was approached by a lad named Mark. He was of mixed origin; his dad was Anglo Indian and his mum was English. He looked me up and down and gave me a look of scrutiny. "I ain't seen you before. You go down the football?" he said. "No, what's that?" I replied. "Filbert Street? Leicester City FC? You're dressed like a trendy. Why? This is the gear that the Baby Squad wear. You can't be dressed like that. You a plastic?" I didn't understand, "A what?" "Look. You can't be dressed like that unless you go to the football. There's a match on Saturday against Birmingham and a load of us are going to represent Leicester. Birmingham have loads of blacks in their firm and they're called the Zulus." "Firm? Zulus?"

Mark gave me a brief outline of what a dresser was and how this uniform was associated with football violence. He said he was recruiting for a new gang of football lads, mainly from ethnic minorities, who could stand and look the part. He wanted my brother and I to join (later named the YTS, Young Trendy Squad). I agreed to be at the train station at 10:30 to travel to Birmingham that Saturday. That morning, I remember putting on the red Fila BJ and standing in the mirror doing karate kicks to the sounds of Man Parrish's

"Hip Hop Be Bop, Don't Stop". I got to the station that October in 1983 and saw an array of lads from all backgrounds wearing a wide range of clobber. I saw differing gangs. Gangs I'd had scuffles with previously when I was with the Asian gangs. I saw the Troopers, the Wongs, the Blues Boys and, of course, the Baby Squad.

I sat on the train where I thought I was the only Asian casual, but I wasn't. There were a couple of other older lads who had done the rounds for many seasons. I didn't feel uncomfortable or any feeling of not belonging. We arrived at New Street station and almost immediately got into a ding-dong with the Zulus. I was in the middle of it, what an electrifying moment! Fear, excitement, adrenaline all mixed together. Sadly, I did not make it to the ground because I was arrested. This was it; this was my calling. I was hooked.

Lez Rotherham – Leeds

It all started for me back in '83. I'd drifted through adolescence following various fashions, like the mod revival and punk scene, but after leaving school and already securing a job (a rarity in those days), things were looking good. I knocked around with a lad who was a mad Leeds United fan who was a year older and worked at the local steelworks. Always smartly dressed in Tacchini tops and bleached jeans with a pair of Adidas Wimbledons. He invited me to my first match in September 1983, Notts County away. I'd managed to rustle up my first casual outfit and we set off.

We boarded the train at Sheffield which was packed with about 150 Geordies. A big lad approached me, Benetton rugby top on. "It's okay," he said, "We're not gonna do you, 150 against 6." We got chatting and went the rest of the day unscathed. I was hooked.

My first week's wages saw an investment in a pair of Lendls followed closely by a pair of Adidas Madeiras.

The scene changed very quickly and the various different phases saw the following: wedge haircut, slicked-back hair, Farah's and crocodile skin loafers, paisley shirts, flared cords, army smocks, Benetton, Armani Kickers, Stone Island, Chipie, Verte Vallee, Fiorucci, Best Company. I enjoyed the shopping expeditions to Manchester and London searching for something a little different. Memorable purchases included a Stone Island fleece from Cody in Plymouth, 1988 for £125, an Armani sweatshirt from Wardrobe in Leeds, 1984 for £35 and a Burberry golfer jacket, 1986 for £84. I'm still paying for it now as my daughter wears it! Green Gazelles and red jeans, Chipie sweatshirt, C17 jeans and red dull Doc Marten shoes from Manchester, nice outfit.

Through the years of following Leeds and hanging about with a lot of lads in Rotherham who entertained a lot of lower league teams, I was always fascinated with what the lads were wearing. Everybody tried to stay one step ahead. Going back to the early days, I remember the rapid pace the casual scene set. When the rave scene arrived, a lot of the lads drifted away from the football scene for the love of ecstasy and fear of long prison sentences under various police operations. Some never returned.

However, in the mid-90s, the casual scene erupted again with a combination of older lads and a new second wave – the next generation (Paul&Shark, Aquascutum, Burberry, Prada, Armani and CP Company) was more evident and to this day seems to be the uniform of the casual. I started going back to football a few years ago, mixing old casual and newer stuff together. My own opinion is the market is flooded with gear all too easy to purchase now. So, purchases like a Berghaus polar cap from the Help the Aged shop for £6 are relished.

I don't follow the fashion or the label. I go for what I think looks good. A few vintage Pringles and Lyle & Scotts adorn the wardrobe next to Aquascutum, MA Strum and CP. One "look" and sight I will never forget is being stood outside the Prince of Wales in Leeds, one cold, Saturday afternoon. A thousand or so members of the Zulu gang disembarked at the train station. Mostly black lads, mostly over six feet tall and mostly wearing ski coats, ski hats, flared cords and jeans and Adidas. Pompey also fetched a massive mob of well-dressed lads and Millwall always look good when they turnout. It's great to share the memories, lads.

Keep it casual. Lez Rotherham, the best dressed kid in town.

Colin J – Millwall

When Celtic won the European Cup in 1967, they were the first British team to do so. As painful as this may be for someone that despises Celtic as much as I do, I grudgingly respect the fact that all but two members of the fifteen-man squad were born within ten miles of Celtic Park. Furthermore, Bobby Lennox was born thirty miles away and Tommy Gemmell was born in Motherwell, just eleven miles away. I don't know where these players were living when they won the European Cup but more than likely they were living in or near the city of Glasgow, and probably not too far from the fans that idolised them. Maybe not in dilapidated East End tenements but suffice to say not in the kind of luxurious, gated mansions even your average, modern-day footballer lives in today. This wouldn't have been unique in that era. For generations, football clubs were the heart of their community. Grounds were usually centrally located, close to the centre of town and often in run-down, working-class parts of town.

Each football club acted as a representative of their town or city and the fortunes of the club could, and did, determine the fortune of the town or city. Or perhaps it was the other way round – such was the importance of each club to its local community. Anyone that had the misfortune of watching televised football during the COVID pandemic in 2020 will appreciate that professional football isn't just about the players. Professional football without the fans is, in my humble opinion, simply worthless. And by fans I don't mean "customers". I don't mean television subscribers, the devotee that streams live games from his armchair somewhere in the world, the casual fan that watches a game in the pub, mindlessly repeating generic drivel spouted by yet another mind-numbingly dull pundit. Or the major tournament "football's coming home" chanting idiots you see in the pub every four years throwing beer over each other and going "mental". And I certainly don't mean the Premier League tourists and their horrendous friendship scarfs. Or the modern-day iPad carrying, popcorn munching newbie.

I'm talking proper fans – those that go to games, week in, week out, home and away. And more importantly, those that went week in, week out, home and away when it wasn't fashionable to do so. And downright dangerous too. Those that traipse up and down the country following their team, irrespective of whether they might see their team win. The faces, the regulars, the die-hards, the people whose names you don't know but you've nodded at in pubs, train stations or service stations up and down the country for years. The "real" fans. The lifeblood of each club.

A number of years ago I read an interesting fact somewhere on the internet, the result of a survey. The accuracy may be dubious but it struck a particular nerve with me: "Millwall have the largest proportion of fans that regularly walk to home games". Given the number of professional football clubs in close knit northern towns, I found this quite remarkable, but it immediately struck a nerve with me and reminded me of why I fell in love with this unique and infamous little football club so many years ago.

I was born and bred in an affluent Surrey town, just south of London. My dad didn't like football – he thought it was a game for melts. Boxing was for real men. My two older brothers had no interest in the game either. I had no guidance about who to support and why. But I loved football. I loved playing it, reading about it, watching it and strangely listening to it on the radio. Bryan Butler and Peter Jones on Radio Two, bringing mid-week European glory nights into my bedroom. Liverpool mainly, but also Forest, Villa and Ipswich. Even Aberdeen and Dundee United. Those marvellous FA Cup finals of the late 70s to early 80s. Such excitement – a whole day of football on the television once a year. It was a big occasion.

Most of all, I loved the Home Internationals. My Dad is Scottish and although he had no interest in football, each year we'd sit down together and he'd cheer Scotland on when they played England. I was too young to remember the infamous 1977 match but I do recall John Robertson scoring the winning goal in the 1981 clash. And I recall Wembley once again being a sea of tartan.

My parents were divorced and in 1983, my dad moved to Catford in South East London. He worked in New Cross, just opposite Goldsmiths College. Alternative weekends were spent in London and more often than not I'd be plonked at a table with my little sister in various New Cross pubs with just a can of coke and a packet of crisps to keep us entertained. I loved it and my little sister loved it too. I loved the people in the pubs, the cigarette smoke. I loved the shellfish and roast potatoes on a Sunday lunch time.

Every pub just seemed so full of characters. Wide boys, gangsters, eccentrics, misfits. We would drink with a Ugandan who may or may not have been a prince. A fella who routinely dressed as a pirate and cultivated his own s**t to grow vegetables. There were non-stop stories, fun and laughter. Tony Sullivan, the writer of *Only Fools and Horses*, once stated that he was inspired to write the hit comedy series based on the characters he grew up with in South East London pubs. That part of South East London had a unique character, even by London standards, and it was that character that gripped me from an early age.

At the heart of New Cross was Millwall Football Club. I didn't know too much about the club when I was twelve and they became my new "local" club. I hadn't heard Peter Jones mention them too often on Radio Two on those big European nights. But the mid-80s are now looked back on as perhaps the peak of organised football violence and whilst Millwall weren't doing so well on the pitch, off it they were at the top of their game. Some of these fellas that were building this fearsome reputation would drink in the same pubs that I was growing up in. I was intrigued. I felt part of

South East London. I felt part of Millwall. And nearly forty years on, I still do.

By the time I was fourteen, I'd been going to football with my mates for a year or so and had already been to many of the London grounds to watch various games involving different teams, but I hadn't been to The Den – and strangely, I couldn't even work out where The Den was or how to get there. That would prove to be an issue for many away fans over the years! I knew it was in New Cross and less than a ten-minute walk from the pubs we were using. On match day, I'd see Millwall fans in the pubs and walking to the games.

In 1985, I recall Leeds fans throwing bananas at our friend, the Ugandan prince. I'd located the ground in the A-Z that my dad had in his car. I wanted to go and experience it for myself. I'd planned the route from the pub to the ground but just needed to get a ticket. This wasn't so easy at the time due to restrictions that were temporarily in place after trouble at the Leeds game that season. However, my Ugandan prince saved the day (perhaps his royal connections extended to the Millwall ticket office) and he managed to get me and a friend a pair of tickets for my first match at The Den in the 1985/86 season, aged just fifteen. A third round FA Cup tie against Wimbledon. Well, if the New Cross pubs were full of interesting characters, the halfway line was at another level completely.

pubs were full of interesting characters, the halfway line was at another level completely.

I was hooked from the minute I set foot in the place. Absolutely smitten. I loved football, I loved the bleakness and hostility of The Den. As hostile as it was to outsiders, the humour, the warmth and the camaraderie of those on the halfway was what I loved the most. I felt at home, secure and safe. Everyone seemed to know each other. Perhaps by today's standards, the humour was politically incorrect and the language a little industrial, but I loved it. I also loved the sinister side of it. The Den was an intimidating place for outsiders to visit and to say there was an edge to it in the mid-80s would be somewhat of an understatement.

Football was on its knees in 1985. There had been a series of serious incidents at various matches home and abroad culminating in the Heysel disaster in May 1985. The tabloids were up in arms and football fans were public enemy number one. Whilst you'd think Liverpool fans would be the outcasts – after all, they had been responsible for thirty-nine deaths – the real enemy of the state, public enemy number one (to this day), were those scumbags at Millwall. Those that had dared to attack the police on the pitch at the Luton FA Cup match in March 1985. The footage of police officers running for their lives had embarrassed the establishment. The tabloid press love to demonise certain groups of people and Millwall fans were once again fair game. I soon learnt a valuable life lesson – a significant amount of people are totally influenced by what they read in the media and can be manipulated into believing whatever the media tell them to believe.

Us Millwall fans will be the first to tell you that fake news was alive and well long before Donald Trump brought it to the attention of the masses. The 1985 media hatchet job followed on from the furore caused by the 1977 *Panorama* exposé of the hooligan element that was an integral part of the club. Millwall fans were demonised as thugs, a perception that has never gone away. Whilst I recognised that Millwall had a serious and justified reputation at that time, a reputation that I was strangely proud of, I would also spend my time defending the fans to outsiders. Millwall fans were fiercely passionate and loyal, respectful, funny and warm. They stood their ground, stood by each other and wouldn't be bullied. They were traits that I loved. They were the embodiment of South East London.

I soon started following Millwall regularly and strangely enough, it coincided with a sudden up-turn in the club's fortunes. Perhaps I was their lucky mascot.

We were promoted to the top tier of English football for the first time in our history on a glorious day in Hull in May 1988. A week later and there was a huge knees up on the Old Kent Road after we'd played Blackburn. But you can't have a good old Millwall knees up without a good punch-up (copyright Harry the Dog) and I recall the mood turning nasty as the party went on into the night, culminating in running battles with the police outside The Victoria pub on Pages Walk. At one point, the police were cowering in a riot van as it was rocked from side to side by hordes of jubilant Millwall fans. Our first season in the top flight was an unbelievable time – top of the league in October and undefeated until we came unstuck in the mud at Ayresome Park at the end of that month. The second time we'd come unstuck that day!

I was a regular – home and away – and loved every minute of it. That same month, I made the relatively short journey to Gillingham for a night match in the League Cup and saw yet another Millwall victory. After the game, I recall an uneventful police escort back to the train station before being herded onto a dirty, cold British Rail rattler back to London Bridge. As the train made its way through North Kent and into South East London, stopping at every stop along the way, no one alighted. Then we pulled into New Cross Gate and the train emptied. Next stop was London Bridge and the last few remaining fans left the train to complete their journey home. I went one step further to Waterloo East and I was totally alone. Even on the main Waterloo concourse there were no other Millwall fans. No one was heading out of London into the Home Counties. They had all got off at New Cross and walked home.

The next home game was against Clough's Nottingham Forest. It remains one of my favourite games at The Den. Still unbeaten, we found ourselves 2-0 down to a decent team and it looked like our unbeaten run was at an end. And deservedly so too. But then Neil Ruddock came off the bench with about ten minutes to go. The impact was immediate and suddenly we were attacking Forest with criminal intent. When Sheringham pulled a goal back, the place erupted. After the initial goal celebrations died down, the noise intensified to a level I'd not heard before. The Lions roared and when Ruddock powered home a header right at the death, the celebrations were insane. "Absolute limbs" as the modern-day fan would say online. The Forest fans weren't happy and we made our way to the waste ground behind the away end to see what was happening. A little mooch on the lookout for trouble – well, I was seventeen. On this occasion, everyone seemed to be in too good a mood for the usual shenanigans. I noticed a little "firm" of Millwall heading towards Bermondsey that looked like they were up to no good and tagged along to see what they were up to. But, as we walked, small groups headed off into pubs or into estates and before I knew it, we were alone in Bermondsey. This wasn't a mob – just a small group of Millwall fans walking home from the game. A scene that would have been replicated in New Cross, Peckham, Deptford etc. after every home game.

When I read that survey about Millwall having the largest proportion of fans that walk to home games, I got to thinking about those two innocuous incidents from 1988. Millwall really were a small, local, community club. Our support came from a very small corner of South East London – from New Cross, Bermondsey, Deptford, Walworth, Peckham, Camberwell and Rotherhithe. Predominantly white working class, historically from families of dockers. Hard working, honest people with morals and unwritten codes. I use the term "honest" loosely as there was a ridiculously high proportion of men within that community who weren't exactly honest, in the true sense of the word. South East London was a criminal hotspot, gangster central. The higher up the criminal ladder you were, the more respect you got. The police were hated, grasses certainly not tolerated. Very similar to the East End of London in so many ways. Obviously, we hated West Ham but the truth was both clubs were very similar at the time – community clubs representing their manor. And these were really, really tough manors. West Ham had Canning Town, we had Bermondsey. The characteristics of the people from these tough communities were virtually identical.

Despite the similarities, there was a deep-seated hatred of those from across the water and never more so than when the two clubs met, providing the perfect opportunity for those from South East London to confront their adversaries from the East End. It wasn't just football. It was so much more than that. Those fixtures were pure evil. The 1987 Simod Cup game at West Ham was the most intense, evil atmosphere of pure hatred that I have ever experienced at football. As a caveat though, I must confess I've never been to a Brighton versus Crystal Palace "derby"...

It can be no coincidence that Millwall and West Ham were two of the top football firms at a time when football violence was at its peak. South East London and East London, perhaps more so than any other parts of the capital, were such historically tough areas. Football violence was tribal and in tough, inner city areas that sense of tribal pride in your manor was tangible; and the football clubs, both West Ham and Millwall, were at the heart of their communities. High-density, rundown housing estates, an abundance of pubs, real poverty, a sense of being born on the wrong side of the tracks, a working-class "f**k 'em all" spirit, an in-built suspicion of authoritarian figures and symbols. All of these factors put together were synonymous with the character of the areas, and in the heart of those communities were the football clubs. Where is that character now, more than thirty years on? What impact has it had on the two football clubs?

The mid to late 80s seem like a lifetime ago now and sadly London has changed beyond recognition. Many would argue not for the better. London may be the capital of England but it no longer feels like an English city. Vast swathes of it are now totally unrecognisable to what they were in the 80s.

The match day experience at football now bears no resemblance to what it was like in the 80s. There is no longer an expectation of trouble in or around the match and of course that should be welcomed. But you know what? I miss it. I'm fifty now and if football violence was still relevant, I like to think I wouldn't get involved. Not that I was ever massively involved when I was younger but if it was there, I embraced it. It added to the atmosphere. I do miss the tribalism and the hostility and I hate the watered-down version that you witness at football now.

There has been the odd occasion in recent years where the adrenaline kicks in. Everton at home in the FA Cup being a prime example. We knew they'd come down, Everton always do. We have history together dating back to 1974. Both sets of fans have long memories. I was drinking in Bermondsey that day in a pub full of lunatics when we got news that Everton had landed at Surrey Docks. Shame it wasn't Bermondsey as expected but never the less, credit for making it on to the manor with real intent. The pub instantly emptied and I grabbed my coat ready to go – but then I realised I was with my son. Did I really want to get involved? Yeah, perhaps! Did I want to drag my eighteen-year-old son in to it? Absolutely not. So, the decision was made to stay in the pub. And five minutes later, the pub was packed again. The police had blocked Southwark Park off so no one could get there anyway. Which was a shame because it would have put an instant stop to the ridiculously biased version of events that Everton fans have spread across the internet ever since. Of course, a few young'uns still try to keep the football violence scene going but I go with my son now and even he grasps that it's a mug's game these days.

I'm not interested in getting involved in any violence. I like the clothes, the trainers, the drink, the day out. Even the travelling. But I'm no longer that interested in the football. The grounds are largely identikit soulless arenas in nondescript parts of the town and when I do go, I tend to leave the game not too long after I've caught up with a few friends at halftime. I still love Millwall and always will. They're an integral part of my personality, the name tattooed on my skin.

John D – West Ham

John Dillane, 57 Forest Gate E7. Raised Irish Catholic with strict parents, the youngest of seven. My first game I can't remember; I was too young. Probably five years old. I remember being told by my eldest brother on the way that our floodlights were the most powerful in the world. Was that true? They had that blue haze about them.

My first away game, I definitely remember – 1968 at Highbury. A cousin who came to stay at our house for the weekend whilst on leave from the RAF took me and my brother. We called for my friend Billy on the way and his mum let him come with us. My cousin was only eighteen, my brother eleven, Billy and I six. I'll add now that my cousin was from Ireland so had not spent much time in London. What was Billy's mum doing, allowing him to come with us? Oh, and we went in the North Bank. Anyone remember the cells at Highbury? It was also the first time I can remember being on the

Underground. I only found out last year it was Billy's first ever West Ham match. He is still a season ticket holder today. Sorry, Billy.

When I was old enough to start going on my own, aged ten or eleven, straight from playing football for the school with a few teammates, I was hooked. By the time I was thirteen, away games, especially in London, were a regular occurrence. I remember being on the District line with a few of my mates and a couple of older boys that Billy was knocking about with. As the train approached Mile End station, one of the older boys warned us to behave as the Mile End Mob would be getting on. He was bang on, the doors opened and on they swarmed – lots of skinheads, really loud but West Ham. We were good boys but this lot didn't give a f***! It made you feel different, part of something, something really different, really good. It taught us to stick together and know when to shut up, respect the elder ones, look after the young ones. Stick together no matter what.

Home match days about the time when we were thirteen years old, Nicky Williams called for Nick O'Connell. They called for me, and we then all went to Eammon Shanahan, onto Ticky Hoy and his older brother Tommy, Jimmy Lynn, Manny Riley, older Kenny

Bedminster and Dennis Johns. All on foot, walking through the back alleys behind the Green Street shops. Good honest fun, banter, stick. I took the most but I had long ginger hair, what did I expect? We caused no trouble, never really had any, but we stuck together. That feeling you'd never know unless you did it.

As soon as we were seventeen and had a licence, we started driving to games. Our map guide was the four lines printed in the programme from the home match before. No sat nav, but we always found our way. The football specials (how f***ing special) run by the travel club were always great fun. Bigger groups of us in the same carriage or compartment, loads of booze. The banter and abuse flying about was relentless (yes, I still had a bit of my ginger hair left, so took plenty). It was fantastic getting off the train in some far-flung place with your mates, and a full train made you feel invincible – nothing could stop us!

It was on one such trip I met my future wife. Yes, Sunderland away 1981, a 2-0 win. It's all been downhill since.

Millie D – West Ham

Despite my parents' best efforts, I didn't take to the beautiful game from childhood. West Ham was in my blood. Mum and Dad met away at Roker Park, cheering on their side. My two older brothers, Declan and Kieran, lived and breathed for the team. I did adopt my family's competitive spirit. I wore my Doc Marten's kit with pride. I liked a kick-about in the garden, but I'd scrunch my face up at the idea of enjoying football.

I didn't enjoy spending my Sundays in a field watching my brothers play, but felt immensely proud and happy when they won, and was lucky enough to witness Kieran scoring direct from a goal kick, in full knowledge of how spectacular that was.

Thinking back to when I was young, I owe football and West Ham a lot. My nan would come and watch every game my brothers played, armed with a flask of hot chocolate and a pot of Haribo hidden beneath a layer of grapes. It meant I saw my nan every week, without fail. When Mum, Dad and the boys would go to Upton Park, I got to have a day with Nan, knowing I'd have a brilliant time, being spoilt rotten. If not with Nan, I'd spend match days with some of my aunts – which guaranteed fun, a pleasure not nailed-on for the die-hard fans of the Boleyn Ground. I was too young at the time to understand why it was a bad idea to rave about my day to the household upon their return from the heartbreak of the 2006 FA Cup final. If I had gone with them, I wouldn't have these treasured moments with my wider family.

I went to Upton Park only once; I must have been about three. We scored and my dad lifted me high above his head in celebration. I cried. A rare occasion occurred where neither my nan nor any of my aunts were able to look after me for the day, so I accompanied the gang to the 2005 victory parade to mark West Ham's return to the top-flight. I was wearing a pair of shoes and it felt that I had not taken them off since I got them. For some reason that day, they rubbed horrible blisters. I associated this pain with the club for years to come.

I always enjoyed the camaraderie of football. For the 2006 World Cup, we built a fort by putting our sofas together & my dad would march us around the garden, banging a plastic tub with a mop to "Vindaloo", the latter resurrected for Russia 2018. Yet I still complained about the noise as they cheered on the boys.

My brothers and I started to grow up, our shared interests began to fade. However, I observed the eternal bond between them and my parents: West Ham. An undying commitment they could always fall back on. I understood the value of this common ground and wanted to be a part of it. I was seventeen, at home with Declan, Mum and Dad were in their old seats at Upton Park, Kieran was in a pub in Bristol while at university; we all shared the elation of Winston Reid's header to win the final game at the Boleyn Ground. I jumped into my brother's arms and he twirled me around the room.

From there, I watched a couple more games from "the year we were good" before getting invested in the 2016 Euros. My first taste of gut-wrenching disappointment: using a month's worth of data watching the Iceland game on my phone.

I was excited for the stadium move. The first game I went to see live since the tear-inducing match in my youth was Wednesday 21st September, a chilly night at home to Accrington Stanley in the third round of the League Cup. We won 1-0 thanks to a Payet free kick in the ninety-seventh minute. The rest, as they say, is history.

I attended nearly all the games of the '16/'17 season and have been a season ticket holder since '17/'18. I am proud to say, no matter the result, no matter the performance, I have never left before the final whistle – always with the team through the good times and the bad.

To me, West Ham is family. The family that gives more time and money to their local community than any other in England. The family that makes you feel safe. If you're a Hammer, someone's always got your back – the claret and blue army look out for each other. Every match, I wear my colours from head to toe: clothes, make-up, nails. I work in the city, and travel to the ground on my own for weekday matches under the lights, meeting my folks at Stratford. On the train, you spot one of your own, and they give you a slight nod and smile. From that point onwards, you know that if something happened, football related or not, they would be there for you no matter what. The family that came together, staff, players, fans, to help a beautiful little girl in need of our help – Isla.

West Ham fans don't take themselves too seriously. They are passionate, ambitious, yet grounded. They just want their team to put a good shift in on the pitch, as they do in the stands. They also have a fantastic sense of humour. The first away game I went to was at Arsenal in the quarter final of the League Cup. It was one of the worst games of football I have ever seen. Ninety minutes – 1 shot on target, 1-0 win to the home side. We stayed solid by sacrificing all attempts at an attack. We were awarded a free kick. It went wide. We all chanted in celebration, "We've had a shot". A month later, we got up early on a grey, drizzly and all-round bleak day – a sign of what was to come. Away at Wigan in the FA Cup, a team two divisions below us. Obiang was stretchered off. Masuaku got a straight red, and an extended ban from the FA the following day. We were 1-0 down and a chorus erupted, "It's only one nil, it's only one nil. How shit must you be? It's only one nil." I was confused – I felt such disappointment and anger, yet I couldn't help but have a smile on my face. These people had seen it all before and knew that if you didn't laugh, you'd cry.

My eldest brother and I have made it a tradition to go to the pre-season matches in the UK. We had Craven Cottage rocking this season, totally outnumbering the home fans. A solid ten minutes of the *Chitty Chitty Bang Bang* rendition of "Bubbles", each round faster and louder left the stand ecstatic – a performance acknowledged with smiles and waves from the players whilst the ball was in play.

One of the funniest moments I've witnessed was away at Ipswich. We'd sold every ticket for this beautiful summer day. A chance to see our new signings and the start of Pellegrini's reign. The ground went silent. One man stood up, and yelled at the top of his voice, "You're just a shit town in Norwich, shit town in Norwich." Two more rounds and the rest of the stand was harmonising, with such a simple yet grating burn against the home side. It was pure brilliance.

As were the celebrations following our 1-0 win against Spurs in 2017. For the second season in a row, they had a chance of winning the Premier League title but needed to beat an under-performing London side to do so. The year before, a game against a Chelsea side who finished tenth, ended in a 2-2 draw, nine bookings for Spurs (a PL record) and a physical rift in the tunnel after the match. Leicester would become champions. On a crisp Friday night, floodlights glowing, Lanzini's sixty-fifth minute strike left West Ham as winners and Chelsea four points clear with a game in hand. Cue verses of, "They've done it again, they've done it again. Tottenham Hotspur – they've done it again." I looked to my left as "Twist and Shout" bellowed from the sound system – my dad was doing just that. His cheeky smile so jubilant, mirrored on Mark Noble's face during his post-match interview. A triumphant grin rekindled from childhood. Both chant and reaction have made starring appearances on every occasion we've beat Spurs since – away in the League Cup the following season, winning 2-3 after being 2-0 down at halftime, and of course, the maiden win by an away side at their new ground. A dominant display for the history book, an unforgettable celebration from Antonio (it should be noted he gives himself a lot to live up to in that department) and as ever, the blissful smirk of Mark Noble following a commanding captain's performance for his childhood club.

West Ham has produced memories I will never forget. The first match after Payet declared he no longer wanted to play for the club. A 3-0 win against Palace, three assists for Antonio who was ill the day before, chants of "he's one of our own" aimed at James Thompkins after he created one of those assists despite being the opposition; a fantastic team performance topped with the cherry of Andy Carroll's stunning bicycle kick. I had the most perfect, side-on view to the best goal I have ever seen live. Obiang's jolting rocket against Spurs, cancelled out but not overshadowed by a similar hit from Spurs' Son. Declan Rice's first goal for the club, a beautiful finish to a superb assist from Nasri. The final piece of a derby we had in our pocket throughout. A wave of maternal love filled me to the brim as Rice watched the replay of his goal on the big screen at the end – his beaming smile unmasking his maturity, a sudden reminder of his youth. Moments like that are rewards for going every week, always believing you can win but with no assurance of points until the full-time whistle sounds.

Mandy D – West Ham

I started going to Upton Park by chance really. I had always loved playing football and supported West Ham like the rest of my family. One day, my dad came by on his way to the match to see if either of my brothers fancied going with him. They didn't, so I piped up, "I'll come with you". And the rest, as they say, is history.

It was the 1974-75 season and we beat Leicester 6-2. I loved it and hardly ever missed another home game for the next twenty-five years. It was great because it forged a bond between me and my dad which had not existed before and I lived from one home match to the next. We always stood in the same place each week, in the Chicken Run, and made friends with the people around us. There was Doreen and Dave the undertakers, who would bring coffin liners to place on the wall to sit on, Pat and Terry and their two boys, and Steve, a family friend.

Dad and I would do the occasional away game which I found such an adventure. We would fly my scarf out of the window and acknowledge fellow supporters on the motorway. My mum worked in the White Hart in Hornchurch and some of the players drank there regularly. She told them about how fanatical I had become, and John McDowell managed to get us two tickets for the FA Cup semi-final at Villa Park. We didn't manage to make the final, but I watched it at my dad's house, and we had a great time. I was lucky in the ballot in 1980 and went to the semis and the final, even took my mum to those as Dad said you see more on the TV.

As soon as I left school in 1979 and started earning, I wanted to get to as many away games as I could. I decided at the beginning of the 1980-81 season that I would do all forty-two league games and all Cup games, home and away. Unfortunately, my brother also decided to get married in May 1981 which caused some arguments in the family. The wedding was scheduled to clash with the last home game of the season, and I was to be maid of honour. I told them that I wouldn't be able to come as I was confident that we would be presented with the Division 2 winner's trophy that day and I had pledged to do every game. Everyone was really angry with me and tried to convince me to change my mind, but I was adamant. In the end, they changed the date of the wedding. It then clashed with the England versus Scotland match, but I didn't say anything. I went on to complete five seasons without missing a single game home or away.

I sometimes went on the football specials and sometimes on Lacey's coaches. My poor mum used to worry as I always went on my own. I was once the only girl on a coach to Newcastle. I remember the lads all passing round a carrier bag to wee in and then as one of them went to throw it out of the door, someone shouted, "Save the bag." He held onto the bottom of it and all the contents splattered along the windows as we drove along the motorway. That was the same day that the Geordies threw the petrol bombs into our enclosure. I promised Mum that I would get tickets in the stands after that.

At the beginning of the next season, September 1981, I set off for an away match at Sunderland. I got chatting to a couple of girls on the train and we stood together inside Roker Park. Then a group of lads behind us started making conversation and we saw them on the train on the way home following our 2-0 victory (Cross & Goddard). The next away game, I was sitting on the train on my own and the boys went past and banged on

175

my window, signalling for me to join them. I travelled with them regularly after that and discovered that a couple of them stood in the Chicken Run so we met at home games too. After a few more weeks, I arranged to go out for a drink with one of them and thirty-eight years and three children later, we are still going strong!

Following on from our Cup wins in 1975 and 1980 and the League Cup final in '81, John and I thought that we were going to spend years enjoying further success but as we all know, it never happened. This hasn't stopped us from inflicting the same lifetime of disappointment on our kids, two of whom still attend regularly with us. But still, at least when we do have a big win, we all really enjoy it.

As frustrating as it can be to support West Ham, I love that we are all in it together, not just my family, but all the friends we have made from following them all over the country. As soon as you get in the pub before a game, you feel part of a private club. For John and I, it has been great to share our passion for the Hammers, no conflict in our household over the footie. I have a friend who follows Manchester United and over the years it has been a fairly successful time for them. On the famous day when Tevez kept us up, we were all indoors watching it and jumping around the room at the final whistle. An amazing day. A short while after the match, my friend was at the door with a bottle of fizz for us. She said that she was pleased for us that we had stayed up as she knew how much it meant to us all. She also told us how much she envied us as a couple because her husband did not follow football and she never had anyone to enjoy it with. I can't imagine being with someone who didn't share my obsession with West Ham. I don't think we would have lasted long if John had not been as mad as me!

Drayton – Portsmouth

1971, my first memory of a visit to Fratton Park. I'm certain I'd been before, but Arsenal at home in the FA Cup is my first memory. Little old Pompey were drawn at home to the mighty Arsenal, tickets were like hot cakes, and 42,000 were squeezed into Fratton Park that day. I walked to the ground with my dad, who was a butcher at the time and somehow managed to get the day off. I was eight at the time, and couldn't sleep properly for days before, excited about my impending visit. It felt like forever queuing up to get into the ground, but once inside, it took my breath away. Running up the crumbling concrete stairs to reach the top of the terrace, my old man shouted at me to slow down, but I wasn't having any of it. I couldn't wait to reach the top and look down at the magnificent view before me. Forty-two thousand fans crammed shoulder to shoulder. The noise was deafening, "Pompey, Pompey" was the shout, followed immediately by

"Arsenal, Arsenal" from the "enemy" crammed behind the Milton End goal. For eighty-eight minutes, the match itself is a distant blur. Arsenal had taken the lead and looked to be heading into the next round, until that is, two minutes from time. Mike Trebilcock picked up a loose ball on the edge of the box and rammed it into the top corner in front of the Fratton End goal, sending the Pompey fans into ecstasy... Well, that's how I remember it anyway, although having watched it many times since, the reality was that Trebilcock's equaliser was a three-yard tap in.

The replay at the famous Highbury was a few days later, again Dad took a day off work and we went up on the train. Two things stand out in my memory of that day. The first was Charlie George diving for a penalty, and helping Arsenal beat Pompey 3-2. The second memory I have is of an Arsenal fan spitting on my dad's Donkey jacket, and my dad turning around and lumping the fella. The police, much to my relief, turned up quickly and dragged the Arsenal spitter out of the ground, after being told by several other fans that it was the Arsenal fan that caused the problem.

Like most football fans, I grew up supporting the team my dad followed. After all, it would be rude not to support the team your dad took you to watch every other week as a kid. The build-up would start on the Monday before the following Saturday's match. I couldn't concentrate at school all week. My only thoughts were about going to Fratton Park to watch my beloved Portsmouth play. As a team, we were s**t to be honest, but the buzz about playing Tranmere or Newport County at home was as big for me as a fan of a United or a City would get about watching their team play a top of the table clash.

Fast forward a few years. I was about thirteen, maybe fourteen, at Reading away. A few of us fresh-faced kids from the local council estate decided to travel up. My first real experience of an away day without supervision. We had no money between us. Well, certainly not enough to pay our way that day, so we bunked the train. One of the fresh-faced kids in our group stole some cans of cider and it didn't take us novices long to get pissed on them. We arrived at Reading station and the hairs on the back of my neck stood on end at the hundreds of Pompey lads getting off the train. Older lads, long hair, flared trousers, starred tank top jumpers. Even at my young age, I felt part of something and loudly joined in with the "we are evil" chant. The walk to the ground was memorable, a long road, and f**k me what happened along that road was pure destruction. Mobs of Pompey everywhere turning cars over, smashing windows, running battles with the police. At first, it was scary but it soon gave me a buzz that stayed with me all my Pompey following life. The game was just as eventful, not for what happened between the teams on the pitch (I honestly can't even remember the score) but for what happened between the fans on the pitch. Several times during the match, the ref took the players off after pitch invasions by the Pompey mob. The match ended, and the journey back to the station mirrored earlier events.

We got to the station and the Old Bill were checking tickets on the train. Me and my pals had bunked on and got our names and addresses taken, but presumably because of our young age, we were allowed to stay on the train. I didn't think any more of it until the next day, Sunday, dinnertime. Sat down with the old man about to have our roast, when there was a knock on the door. My dad got up to answer it – it was the local police. I overheard him telling my old man that I'd been reported for bunking the train the previous day and drinking underage. Knowing what my dad was like, I f**ked off to my bedroom not wanting the belt from him for my adventure the previous day. I heard the front door shut and waited nervously for his reaction.

I wasn't disappointed as the bedroom door flew open and he stood there with his belt in hand. I got a right hiding, but not for my antics. The hiding was because when he was at the door talking to the copper, our dog had jumped up on the kitchen table and eaten his roast dinner. He didn't give a toss about what happened the previous day, but was more concerned with the mutt scoffing his Sunday roast. I've been in a hundred football related adventures since, but that one memory will never fade. Just another memory that made me fall in love with my club even more.

Fashion became a massive part of football, especially in the late 70s. A pub smack-bang in the middle of a Portsmouth council estate, called The Havelock was frequented not just by the local estate lads, but from lads all over the city, famously went on to be known as The Havelock Boys. It was my first taste of fashion, other than the flared trousers and tank tops of the mid-70s. If you walked into the pub any night of the week, you would see a boozer full of skinheads. Shaven heads, Fred Perry's, Levi jeans, Doc Martens, Crombie's. Portsmouth was never a city full of trendy fashionable shops. You had to travel out of town to buy some decent clobber. Most of us skinheads trawled around charity shops, where you could occasionally pick up the odd button-down Ben Sherman for a few shillings.

The skinhead scene really took off in Portsmouth during the late 1970s. It was not uncommon to see upwards of a couple hundred skins at Fratton Park. One particular away game up north, the name of the opposition team escapes me now (I've visited way over seventy grounds following Pompey through the years) but hordes of us skinheads were greeted by the northern Old Bill outside the stadium and refused entry until we agreed to remove the laces from our Doc Martens. Looking back, it must have been hilarious watching the post-match ruck and seeing poorly aimed laceless boots flying through the air.

Following Portsmouth all over the country cost me a lot, not just financially, but it also took me away from my family. There were times when following Pompey and getting into scrapes was more important to me than spending time with my loved ones. As any supporter involved in the scene during those days will tell you, it was a drug, the most addictive drug money could buy. Bunking trains up north every two weeks (seven of us to Middlesbrough and back springs to mind, for the cost of a nineteen-pence platform ticket). No matter what, I had to be there. Tranmere away on a Friday night, Stockport away on a Monday night, all equally as important for me to be there, as if it was a Cup final.

I'm well into my fifties now, and although I don't travel away, bar a few games a season, I'm still at Fratton every game. The blood still runs blue. The passion still runs deep. Not just for my football club but for my city. As mentioned above, following Pompey cost me not just money, but my liberty a couple of times as well. Would I do it all again? In a heartbeat.

Grey Wolf – Chelsea

Part I

"Have you ever seen Chelsea win the league?" was a famous chant from away supporters in days gone by, as they sort to belittle Chelsea supporters. I often got strange looks as I would shout back, "Yes, I have," all because of a life-changing birthday present.

Most birthday presents are quite forgettable. Every now and then one comes along that you remember for years. Few, if any, are life-changing. I was lucky enough to have one of the latter. I remember my dad saying we were going to Chelsea for my birthday present. Living at that time in Britannia Road, I felt quite underwhelmed, cheated even. I was looking forward to something I could play with. I was five years old after all. So, on 10th November 1951, my dad and I walked down Britannia Road, and across Fulham Road, and up to the main entrance opposite the Rising Sun pub. I can remember slowly walking up the huge stairs outside the Shed, and thinking, *I wish I was at home playing with a normal present.*

Then, upon reaching the top, I remember looking out across the huge amphitheatre in awe. I'd never seen anything like it. Even the 1951 Festival of Britain on the South Bank a few months earlier didn't have the effect that that moment had on me. It seemed so huge for a five-year-old. The funny thing is that's all I can remember of my first game, apart from the fact I took to the team in blue straight away, and we won 4–2... against Manchester United.

The thing is that in those days Stamford Bridge was like how the Emirates is today: a f**king library. Silent until a goal was scored, then everyone started clapping. It wasn't until a few years later that Ted Blake wrote in the programme that the fans must make more noise. It worked. After 1955, Stamford Bridge came alive with noise.

My most memorable game as a child was when I was eight – Sheffield Wednesday at the Bridge in April 1955. I was standing near the corner flag, where the West Stand meets the Shed (in those days it was the West Terrace). We won 3-0, and at the final whistle, a few people started to leap over the small wall and run onto the pitch. Thinking we had won the League, I took one look at my old man, who was soaking up the atmosphere, and climbed over the wall and followed the crowd. The next thing I heard was, "Come here." I looked around and saw a six foot three inch giant running after me, and quickly took to my heels. Pushing my way through the crowd, I got to the front, and saw the old wooden East Stand, just as the crowd fell into a deadly silence.

An old man (who I now know was Old Man Mears) was standing with his hands up signalling for silence. Then after a short wait, that seemed like hours at the time, he said something on a big old-fashioned microphone. I never heard what because everyone went berserk, jumping up and down, and shouting their heads off. I felt a hand on my shoulder and looked around. It was my dad, who now had a beaming smile on his face. "Manchester United have lost," he said, before shouting at the top of his voice... "We've won the League!"

I retold this story on the Chelsea Chat site back in the 1990s and no one believed it, but then someone posted a film clip from a Pathe Newsreel, and said, "There's a small boy running across the pitch, in the same place you said you ran, have a look." To my amazement, there I was! In the match day programme for the Fulham game in 2005, there was a full-page photo from that day, and to my surprise there I was, right in the front.

I'm now in my sixty-nineth season at Chelsea and it's taken me from Stamford Bridge to most cities in England, and all the cities that we've played in across Europe. Chelsea became an obsession. They were my tribe, and I still drink with friends I made back in 1966 at the League Cup final at Leicester City. I even got to know the team back then as when we played AC Milan in 1965, I went to the replay, and there were only around forty supporters flying to Italy for it. We flew on the same plane as the team and stayed in the same hotel. That never happens today. We won 2-1 at home, and on aggregate that meant a draw, hence the play-off. We drew 1-1, and had to sit on razor blades as they tossed a coin to see who went through. That was nerve racking, but we won the toss, and went through. I always thought that was an unfair way to decide a game, and found out just how unfair when three years later, we drew with DWS Amsterdam at home, lost the toss, and went out. We made up for that in 1971, for after winning the FA Cup for the first time in our history (only the second Cup we'd ever won), we went to Athens and won the European Cup Winners' Cup. I was there for both games; but that's another story.

Part II

Lord Richard Attenborough, Baron Attenborough RIP

I first met Lord Attenborough at the Blue Boar Service Station on the M1 motorway. Having driven from Nottingham after a game at Forest, the Mini (which was sluggish on the way down) refused to start. I was standing there with my best mate Angus looking at the engine, when a voice from behind said, in an immaculate English accent, "Good grief, what do you have there?" "1300 cc with a Roots Supercharger," I replied, turning to see who was so interested in the engine. You could have knocked me down with a feather, for standing there was (the then) Sir Richard Attenborough.

After a short chat about it breaking down, he pointed out that the Supercharger belt was worn and loose, and was probably the cause. I told him the station mechanics couldn't fix it 'till Monday so we were going to thumb a ride back to London. "Oh, no need for that.

I'll give you a lift." "Cheers," said Angus, "Where's your jam jar?" Sir Richard chuckled and said, "Over there," pointing to a Rolls Royce Silver Shadow. My bottom jaw dropped, "You having a laugh? You're Sir Richard Attenborough, ain't you?" A broad grim crossed his face, as he said, "Yes, but we're all Chelsea supporters here, so let's be getting you home."

Climbing into the back seat, I noticed his wife Sheila Sim sitting on the front seat. The Roller pulled out of the Blue Boar, and onto the main drag of the M1, and we started chatting. "Good result tonight," said Sir Richard. "Yeah," I replied. "Two victories in one night is always nice," Sir Richard said. Angus asked, "Oh? What was the other victory?" "You two winning that fight," came the shocking reply. "You saw that?" said Angus in amazement, "Then why are you giving us a lift?" "Because we're all Chelsea!" came the reply.

I met Lord Attenborough a few times again, and he always remembered that night. At the 100-year bash, he called me over, and related the story of that night to the half dozen people he was talking to.

Lord Richard Attenborough, a wonderful, wonderful man, and a true Blue!

RIP

Part III

A group of us from the North Stand (I won't name names, even though there was no trouble, so I'll just invent some) decided to go on the eight-day trip as £70 was a bargain back then. There were a number of different trips, with half-day, whole-day, and I think three-day also. We landed at Athens airport and came out looking for our coach. The eight-day trip meant we travelled over 120 miles to the Gulf of Corinth, and a resort called Loutraki. Back then, it was a small, quiet resort, with around a dozen hotels (looking at it today on Google maps I didn't recognise it as it's grown huge). To the right of the beach was a complex called Poseidon. Once finding our hotels, we all went to one of the welcome parties. They had trays full of Ouzo, the local aniseed spirit. We were warned about drinking too much of it, but after three glasses, I didn't feel any effect at all. So, I had another three. Still with no effect, me and Jock decided to go outside and have a fag. Well, I can remember going through the glass door, and taking the first step. The next thing I remember is waking up in the evening. Jock said I took two steps and just fell flat on my face, unconscious.

What I found good about the food in Greece was that most of us didn't really like it as it's salad based, but I loved it. I'd have dinner in my hotel, then go to the other couple of hotels some of the boys were staying in and have dinner there – the owners were so used to seeing me arrive they thought I was staying with them. The second night there, we decided to go and check out the Poseidon. As we arrived, we discovered it was a German holiday camp and the guys on the front gate were panicking, seeing twenty to thirty English football supporters. Being German, I explained that we were Chelsea supporters, over there for the Cup Winners' Cup final on Wednesday. After ensuring them that we weren't there for trouble, they let us in and we had a great night.

The next day was Tuesday. We all got up early, had breakfast, and went to the town centre to get the bus into Athens to see the team arrive. On reaching the centre of town, we found the bus station, bought return tickets, and boarded the two waiting buses. The 120-mile trip was something to behold. Near Athens, the road goes along the side of a mountain, and the coach was doing seventy miles per hour, just inches away from a steep drop into the Mediterranean Sea. Surviving that, both buses arrived in the centre of

Athens, near Constitution Square. The square is where the Royal Palace is and has a piazza with market stalls where you can buy all sorts of things from souvenirs to food. There were around forty of us, some North Stand, some Shed boys, and a few ordinary supporters making up our numbers.

So, off we walked to get a bus to the airport, and upon arriving were greeted by the Greek police. These were the days of the military dictatorship, and they weren't much loved by the locals, but they were really good to us. A sergeant came over as we were getting off the bus, and told us that as Panathinaikos (a local Athens team) were playing in the European Cup final at Wembley later that month, nearly all the Greeks were supporting Chelsea in the final on Wednesday, so they didn't want any trouble. We said we had no intentions of starting any, we were only at the airport to see the team in. He then told us that the best place to see the plane land was on the terminal building roof, but as no one was allowed up there, we had to be quiet. He then led us up to the roof just as the plane was taxiing towards the terminal. We all stood and waited quietly.

Then the team started to walk down the stairs from the plane to the tarmac and we just couldn't help ourselves. We started up a chorus of "Chelsea! Chelsea!"

The team started waving. David Webb started clowning around, followed by Alan Hudson and Tommy Baldwin. We then rushed down the stairs and into the main lounge to say hello to the team, as we knew many of them from drinking with them in the Ifield pub after games. They were surprised to see us, but were then escorted away to the team coach. We all walked towards the main door of the terminal, to the bus back to Constitution Square. We were met by a bunch of press, who started taking photos of us. Some made the front page of one of their dailies.

Taking a bus from the airport, we passed the Acropolis and Steve and Jock said, "Let's go in there." So, at the bus stop, we all piled off, and walked up to the entrance. The attendants on duty looked like they were going to have a baby when they saw us approaching, and started screaming, "Stop! Stop! You can't come in here!" They explained that the Acropolis is a religious monument, and not a circus attraction. At this point, I should explain that we were all dressed up in Chelsea colours with scarves tied around our wrists, carrying flags. We came to an agreement that half of us would go in, with no flags or scarves, whilst the other half would stay outside. The Acropolis was impressive. The size was something to behold. In photographs, the steps look like you can walk up them, but in real life they are each around six feet high.

Going back to the entrance, we were again greeted by angry attendants because whilst we were in there, those left outside had formed a group near the main gate, and had become a tourist attraction themselves, with Yanks and others photographing them and not the sights to behold. It quickly became clear that the other half of us wouldn't be allowed in, so we walked back down to the stop and boarded a bus to Constitution Square.

Walking over to the bus station, it became clear for the first time that we had unknowingly bought tickets from two different bus companies, and around a dozen of us had tickets for another bus provider. We bid farewell to the others and walked back to Constitution Square. As I said earlier, there were lots of market stalls and tables where you could eat in the open. We started asking people where the bus station was, but no one could speak English, or were too scared to in case the military would come over. So, Jock and I climbed onto a table, pointed to the tickets and started shouting, "Anyone know where this bus station is?" A huge crowd gathered and started blocking part of the main road. At this point, a policeman came over, scattering the locals. I looked at Jock and said, "Shit, we're gonna be arrested."

This prompted Jock to jump down. He asked if the policeman could speak English. Luckily for us, he could. We explained how half of us had one pass, and were on their way back; whilst we had this yellow ticket, and couldn't find the bus station. He said, "It's okay. I'll call my captain and get it sorted out." Still thinking we were gonna get arrested, we thought of doing a runner, but none of us knew where to run, so we stayed put.

After around ten minutes, we heard sirens, and the locals scattered once more. Six Mercedes police cars came screaming into the square, and stopped in front of us. The captain got out and walked towards us, with each one of us thinking we were to go to a Greek jail. "Hello," he said in a cheerful voice, "I hear you're having trouble finding the bus station." Steve said, "Yeah, but we're not causing any trouble. So, why all the police cars?" With a smile, he replied, "Oh, they're here to take you to the bus station." We looked at each other in disbelief. "But what about the flags?" I asked. "No problem," he replied, "Stick them out of the windows."

Well, at this we just looked at each other and laughed, then started tying scarves to the door handles and sticking flags out of the open door windows. Off we set, in the most bizarre police convoy you've ever seen. "Have you seen much of Athens yet?" asked the captain (it was his car Jock, Steve, John and I had got into). "Well, we've seen the Acropolis and the airport, but that's it," I said. "Okay," came the reply, and he got on his radio and said something in Greek. "We're going to go sightseeing," continued the captain.

Next thing we know, the bizarre convoy wound its way through Athens as we got a guided tour of the city. After around twenty minutes, the captain said, "Now, do you want to see something funny?" "Yeah, why not?" said John. The captain put the sirens on as we screeched into the bus station. The locals took flight and ran in all directions trying to get out of the way. Some fell over in their haste, making the captain laugh his head off. The police cars stopped by a coach, and he explained that this was our bus back to Loutraki. When we got out, we noticed heads nervously poking around corners, to see what was going on. "Don't worry about them. They thought we were raiding the place!" concluded the captain with a broad smile. So, we boarded our bus, and went back to Loutraki.

Warren J – Liverpool

I'm a Liverpool Football Club supporter. My first memories of football are from around the mid-1990s. Having passionately followed the sport for two and a half decades since, I have seen and experienced first-hand many changes in the culture of football on the terraces. Also, I've seen the game evolve dramatically in that period, both on and off the pitch.

The first game I can ever remember attending as a live spectator was a Tranmere Rovers match. My uncle took me down to Prenton Park, and little did I realise then that the events I saw unfold before my eyes would fuel my passion for the beautiful game for the next twenty-five years of my life. This game was an absolutely epic encounter, two sides going toe-to-toe against one another. It was almost like a basketball match, you attack, then we'll attack. The game finished four a piece. I can just remember almost instantly getting a feeling of being a part of something. A belonging. Almost like a calling.

By the final whistle, I knew that football would go on to become my passion in life. I can only describe it as feelings of passion, pride and togetherness. I could just immediately sense what football means to people. Football unites so many. People from all walks of life, who are brought together for a common cause; the love and joy of football, of following their team. It's a very tribal experience. You feel a part of a group, like you suddenly belong.

My love for Liverpool FC in particular began when my uncle took me to Ewood Park to see Liverpool play Blackburn Rovers. Although my team lost that match, I could once again feel the emotions and the camaraderie amongst the fans. It didn't matter that we had lost. We were all in it together. We all knew, we'd be going to see the Reds again very soon.

My first taste of football at Anfield, home of Liverpool, was when my father took me to a match against Crystal Palace, around 1997. Liverpool won 2-1. I can remember my dad taking a seat that was "obstructed view", a perfect example of how football has changed in a relatively short time. You wouldn't have this sort of thing happen these days, certainly not in the

Premier League. Anfield was in a period of transition. During my last visit, in 2016, I can remember the stark difference from what it was like then. For example, it had elevators. In the late 90s, there were only stairs! I can also vividly remember the Palace fans chanting some quite vile chants about one of our players at the time, a young Michael Owen.

I'll always remember the sense of fury and subsequent backlash from our supporters. This showed me the culture within the terraces, of standing up for one of your own. It also showed me that football can evoke feelings of not only positive emotions. Rage, fury, and for ninety minutes at least, a hatred of the opposition can also be present. You'd give anything to just win. You become so involved at times, and so much in a zone, that feelings you may not have known you even had just come pouring out. You get involved in the uproar of the whole stadium, when the referee awards a free kick or penalty against your side, for example. It's euphoric and almost gives a feeling of ecstasy, or sometimes relief, when your team scores a goal. It completely contrasts against the pain, the heartache and sheer frustration that's generated when you see your team concede a goal. One change I have noticed relates to this, following the introduction of VAR. I have seen and heard from fellow fans of the frustration this has caused them. Not so long ago, you knew that a goal was a goal, as long as the flag of the assistant stayed down. Nowadays, you are left in limbo, looking at the big screen praying the goal stands.

Football is so much more than what happens within the ninety minutes. It's the whiff of the pie and chips that hits your nostrils as you walk by the stands. It's the electricity in the air when you get hordes of people coming together for a massive game. It's the pre-match and post-match beers with the lads. It's driving up to the game, or taking the train. It's walking up the street and seeing the stadium in the distance, anticipating what lies ahead. This is all a huge part of the experience.

Football, and everything that comes with it, has evolved a lot in my time. The fashion people are wearing at the ground, the songs being sung (which are becoming fewer and further between), the changing face of the stadiums, the changing football programmes. There is just a whole different feel about the atmosphere at the games now. I can remember people saying to myself and a friend to sit down, and to not chant and shout so loudly! This would not have happened when I first started watching. There is more of a family element to it these days, in addition to football becoming more corporate. Often, working-class spectators are priced out of the game. These are some of the major changes I have seen in the last twenty-five years.

There are differences between individual clubs and fan bases too. Some clubs have a real family feel about them, and some give out less of a warmth and togetherness about the supporters. This is influenced by the number of season ticket holders, whether you always sit with the same people, for example. You just make friends because you see these people every week, together through thick and thin. Some clubs have varying songs, some only have a couple. So, I believe the differences between clubs is a big aspect, and a key part of what makes terrace culture so unique. You'll get a different feel and different atmosphere, whichever ground you go to.

I've seen players take the wrath of our own supporters when watching Liverpool. I feel these days that the demands and expectations within the game are so great, that players don't quite get the backing from the stands that they once used to. Players can be vilified by their own supporters when the team is playing badly, particularly players that fans don't feel have the right passion or attitude or fit into the ethos of the club.

Mr Cavener, Ex Pro. Interview

Cavener was born on 2nd June 1961 in North Shields. However, at the age of ten, he emigrated to Australia with his family in the early 1970s. Having made an impression on the pitch down under, Arsenal Football Club offered him a trial at Highbury at the age of fifteen.

After his family relocated to Burnley, he signed schoolboy forms for the Clarets first before signing a professional contract in May 1979. He made his debut for the club against Leyton Orient on 3rd November 1979 and became a regular in the Clarets' first-team squad. The following season (1980-81), he made forty-two appearances, scoring four goals. He lost form the following season and made twelve League and Cup appearances as the Clarets won the Third Division Championship.

After a loan spell at Valley Parade where he made nine appearances for Bradford City, he was released by the Clarets at the end of the 1982-83 season. Cavener then went overseas and joined FK Karlskrona in Sweden where he made just one appearance. He returned to England, signing for Gillingham before becoming a first-team regular at Northampton Town. Here, he returned to Turf Moor to face Burnley in the club's first-ever fourth division match in August 1985.

Cavener joined Kettering Town in the summer of 1986 and was a key member of the Vauxhall Conference side helping them win the Bob Lord Trophy final against Hendon Town at Wembley Stadium. Whilst driving back from the Cup final, he was badly injured in a car accident and spent eight months in hospital, bringing an end to his playing career.

Having joined Arlesey Town as manager, he led them to a League and Cup double in the 1994–95 season, which saw them win the Southern Premier Division with a record 107 points, as well as beating Oxford City 2–1 in the FA Vase final at Wembley Stadium.

Chadwick Media this week caught up with the former Clarets midfielder to speak about his football career and his time at Turf Moor. During the interview, we discussed the people that have influenced his career and the best players he has played with and against over his football career.

Who had the biggest influence on your career in football?

There can only be one person. The biggest influence on my football career was my dad.

What is your best football highlight?

It's difficult to name just one highlight, but three things come to mind. The first would be scoring two goals for Burnley on my away debut in the old second division. The second would be scoring a hattrick in a 3-2 win at Notts County when I was eighteen. And the final thing would be leading Arlesey Town out as manager at Wembley in the 1994-95 FA Vase against Oxford City which we won 2-1. Brilliant day and fantastic bunch of players.

Tell us about your Football League debut?

My League debut was against Leyton Orient at Turf Moor on 3rd November 1979. We lost the game 2-1 and I was very nervous playing on the same team as legends like Alan Stevenson, Keith Newton, Martin Dobson, Brian Flynn, Peter Noble, Jim Thomson, Leighton James, Paul Fletcher, Steve Kindon and many more.

Toughest opponent you faced and why?

Again, it is difficult to pick out just one player. I would say the toughest opponents I faced were Ron Harris, Ray Stewart and Dennis Smith. To be honest, in those days all the fullbacks wanted to give you a hard time and they could get away with kicking and elbowing you. It was nothing like what you see in the game today.

Best goal you scored and why?

I didn't score too many goals, so the two goals I scored against Notts County in my first away game for the Clarets really stand out. The game was played at Meadow Lane in front of a crowd of 7,596 on 29th December 1979. The first goal came on eighteen minutes after beating two men. I shot from fifteen yards into the far corner of the net. The second goal was more of a team effort with Billy Hamilton, Marshall Burke and Derek Scott working hard to put me through on goal to score my second of the game.

Best manager you played for and why?

I liked all the managers I played for in different ways, from Harry Potts, Brian Miller and Frank Casper (Burnley) Trevor Cherry (Bradford City), Tony Barton and Graham Carr (Northampton Town), Keith Peacock (Gillingham), and Alan Buckley (Kettering). All good managers and I learnt from them all over the years.

Best player you played with and why?

Again, tough question. I played with some fantastic players, such as Leighton James. One of the best, he had everything you ever needed in a player. Then there was Martin Dobson, he was such an elegant player. Paul Fletcher, who used to just hang in the air. We also had players, like Steve Kindon, who were fast, direct and so powerful. And Trevor Steven, a brilliant player and I knew when training and playing alongside him, he would go onto big things. Whilst at Bradford City, I played alongside some of the club legends, players such as Bobby Campbell (below), Stuart McCall (current Bradford City manager), Peter Jackson and Mark Ellis. At Gillingham, I played on the same side as Steve Bruce, who was also in the team that I played in at Wallsend Boys Club.

You were part of the Clarets Third Division Championship team under Brian Miller. Could you tell us about that Championship season and squad?

It was an excellent season for the club. However, it was a disappointing season in some ways as I think I only played around six League games. I spent most of the season frozen out as the team were playing well and my form was not the best. I was low on confidence, but the games I did play in I really enjoyed. We had a great trip to Spain at the end of the season to celebrate and the team did fantastic to win the League. It was a top bunch of players.

What was it like playing football in Sweden for FK Karlskrona and how did it differ from the UK?

I was very disillusioned after getting released from Burnley and I had numerous offers, but I had a call from an agent about playing in Sweden. I thought, *Why not?* The problem was before my registration came through, which took three weeks, the team was relegated and I had only played one game. I thought football was great; a lot slower and easier than in the UK.

Anyway, I was asked to go out on loan or they would pay my contract up and I could go home, so I spoke to the PFA and ended up signing for Gillingham.

(I felt it important to get the view of a pro footballer who was about at the time and era this book refers to. An era where you could get away with certain things post-Big Brother. He mentions the Chopper Harrises and Ray Stewarts of this world. These were guys we looked up to. Tough blokes. And when the tackle flew in, the crowd roared. For me, Mr Cavener touches on how you had to put your time in to make ends meet in the game. The battle and physical nature of the game were all part of the culture. Anyone who felt they was a superstar or primidone didn't last long on or off the pitch. No one had time for that back then!)

Chris – Wolves

I first went down the Wolves with my stepdad in 1974 to watch Wolves against Derby. We went regularly throughout the 70s. Wolves were a decent side. My first recollection of some aggravation was when we played Leeds in the FA Cup quarter final in 1977. Fifty thousand fans inside Molineux. I vividly remember fans from both sides being brought down the front covered in claret. It happened against Millwall in the same season. There was only about 300 of them in the bottom left corner of the South Bank, but they were fighting like f**k. It was fascinating for a nine-year-old.

I started to go on my own with a couple of pals when I was about twelve. I saw some older lads from my school in town. I was wearing my mod parka but they dressed differently, tight jeans, cagoule and the now famous wedge haircut. It was about 1981 when I started to try to dress the same way as them. Being only thirteen with a paper round, the clothes were hard to come by. My first casual uniform was a red Slazenger jumper, light blue cords that had to be taken in so they were almost drainpipes and a pair of white and green Puma trainers.

The football firm at Wolves was the Subway Army. Many of whom were from around me in a place called Wednesfield. The younger Subway lads were called the Subway Apprentices. I knew a few of them who to this day are some of my best friends. Back in those early 80s days, if you wanted to know what clothes were "in", you would go down George's Cafe on Linthouse Lane, Wednesfield. The Subway Apprentices would be there. It was a great time for the dresser scene. All the names would be worn there: Pringle, Lyle & Scott, Fila, Lacoste, Ellesse, Tacchini and Benetton with Trimm Trabs, Samba Diadora and Adidas kickers.

If you went in there wearing old clobber, you'd get slaughtered and wouldn't go back until you had the latest gear. Things back then would be in and out of fashion in a matter of months. You had to keep swapping and selling clothes to get the next in. That was about 1982-83.

I remember the 1983/4 season. Wolves had been promoted and our first game was Liverpool at home which was a bad day for the scalls. Some were robbed and stripped. The Wolves mob was massive. We had all the sportswear you could imagine, a well smart crew that day. Two days later, we played Arsenal and that was the end of the sportswear and Pringle for me.

My brother and I were on top of the subway and I think the Arsenal Gooners were standing by the entrance to get in. They were about fifty handed. All of them in quality sportswear. While we were standing watching them, a mob of about forty black and white lads stood on top of the subway. It was Arsenal's main boys, the herd. One of them started to talk to us. He asked who we were and then went on to say the sports gear had gone out and Armani and Cecil Gee were the new fashion; and most of them were wearing it. I had seen about ten of the older Wolves subway lads in similar clothes earlier in the day but I'd thought, *What are they wearing?* Well, after speaking to the Arsenal lads, I knew that was the way forward. At school on the following Monday, I told my pals what I had seen and Fila and Tacchini had gone out. Most of them didn't believe me but after a few months, they knew I was right.

In '83, I met a lad from Salford who was a United fan. From 1983-6, I went to a lot of United games, West Ham, Liverpool, Everton, Villa, Forest, Tottenham, Arsenal.

213

Some really violent encounters. My team Wolves were going down the divisions rapidly and in '83, the Subway Army had finished at Wolves when quite a few of them were jailed after a fight with the Wolves Woolly Backs in town in '82 led to one of them being stabbed to death. So, a few of us from Wednesfield would go to United. I loved the Manc fashion at the time. They would be wearing semi-straight leg jeans, check shirts, round neck jumpers with their United pin badge, sometimes with a tweed blazer and what I used to call the Adidas flat-bottom trainers. I now know them correctly as the City Series, a quality but understated look. Everyone else was wearing Armani and expensive label clothes. Sometimes it was strange being in the United firm because there didn't seem to be anyone leading them. At most clubs, you knew who the main boys were.

In 1986, I was eighteen and the lads I hung around with started to go back up to Wolves. We had reached rock bottom and we were having a bit of success on the pitch so a few more wanted to go. This was to be the start of the third Wolves crew. The mid-to-late 70s had the Temple Street Mob. The late 70s to '83 had the Subway Army and in '86, we were called the Bridge Boys. Granted not the best of names. So, we met up with other lads from around the Wolves area park fields – Bilston, Pendeford, Willenhall – and lads from Stourbridge, Dudley, Telford, Cannock and Kidderminster. For two years, it was a good time going to places you had only seen on the football results. In 1986, I saw a different angle on fashion. Armani and Nike running trainers had gone out. Reebok trainers were the shoe of choice. I remember wearing a pair of check trousers to Rotherham in a Cup match and Wolves got hammered 6-0. As our results got better, more were going and trips to the seaside turned into eventful days and weekends away. Torquay, Southend, Scarborough, all ending in mayhem.

There were some good firms in the lower divisions when we were there. Cardiff, Swansea, Wrexham and Newport – all good mobs. Cardiff one of the best. Tranmere, Port Vale, Lincoln, Stockport and Northampton who we had a good row with in '87 along with some Cockney Reds they had with them. Whilst the team and the lads were making headlines, the plod had taken notice of our exploits. It was the period of the dawn raid and we had one of ours in March 1988. Around sixty-five of us got done, myself and my brother included. We made the national telly as the plod came to my mum's house. The TV cameras came with them so we were on the six o'clock news. It was our fifteen minutes of fame. We were banned from '88-'93 but the rave scene took up our time during the ban. It's well documented that football lads were in warehouses, fields and house parties. A prime chance for a row but we were too loved up for that. I had some great times at the rave scene. Towards the end of 1990, a few of us went to Quadrant Park in Liverpool, or should I say heaven? What a club and what a dove. I went up every Saturday from then to the summer of '91. Great times. I met some great people, some football lads, others just people on the same level.

Football took a back seat for a couple of years. During that time, Stone Island made an appearance. The first time I saw it was on a Cockney Red at Villa Park, at the end of '86. I think his name was Miles. I'd seen him at United a few times. When I asked him what it was, he replied in that Cockney tone, "You'll all be wearing it soon." And how right he was. First, I had a T-shirt and then a couple of jumpers. I used to go to Limeys in Derby for them when they were still reasonably priced. I got a coat from a shop in Luton called Uniform too.

By '92, I thought it had run its course, but how wrong I was. 1994 saw us come off our bans and for most, it was business as usual. Straight back as boys and straight back rowing. Stoke was a great rival for us back then, both at home and away. Always a good day out. The Albion, our nearest rivals, were eventful back then too. Ralph Lauren was a big deal then. Most people I knew had at least one shirt from Bicester but I'd never been. I thought a couple of years previously, Stone Island was just another name in the fashion game. How wrong I was. In the late 90s, it came back with a vengeance and in 2020, it seems to be the football lads' fashion of choice. Other names were just as good in my opinion: Paul&Shark, Prada, Belstaff, Moncler. Canada Goose and Armani still put out some decent gear.

Fast forward to the present and my violent days are long gone but I still like to wear decent clothes and trainers due to the fact I wouldn't know how to dress any other way! So, that's my account of the best times of my life.

Jason Again

Halftime Update and Scores

You see the memories in the entries from childhood upwards, how everything started innocently. And in some instances, not so innocently! But the routes are pretty similar in their content.

The scene at the time was one of limited entertainment, and the physical act of going to a match or event was in itself a major part of the event. The day might start by Uncle John or a big brother/cousin picking you up, getting a bus or train, grabbing a bit of brekkie or a manky burger, then purchasing a scarf or programme or meeting your mates and walking up to the ground together, swapping gossip and stories. You would be in awe at the thousands of people swaying, singing, chanting, ranting, leaving little room for the game. Often, you might not even know the game had started! There would be surges, stampedes, argy bargy and a hundred times you thought that you were going to be lost or trampled but like a magic bungee cord, you were catapulted back to safety to receive a clip round the ear from that uncle or big brother for getting lost. The players would enter the field like Greek gods. You stood opened mouthed as these icons stroked the ball around in their neat clean kits that were later transformed into piles of sludge! The pitch looked pristine and you would often dream that you might one day grace it. Again, an hour later, it would look like a Christmas pudding and the players would hack and skate around in vain attempting to get it up the other end.

In later life, you would marvel at how these geniuses could even stand up, let alone dribble or control the ball, and how such marvellous goals were ever scored in such awful conditions. You would freeze your nuts off, be soaked to the bone, you would eat a rubber-bullet meat pie and drink warm-up piss (aka Bovril). You would hear folk cuss and curse, veins would pop in their necks and they would froth at the mouth. It would be a place no child should ever want to go, but each week, you would beg whoever to take you.

When it was an away game, you were lost. You were too young and big bruv would go with his mates and would promise he would take you when you were older, trying to put you off by painting a picture of a northern town somewhere where they eat little kids for breakfast, and men were men and so were the women (no offence to our northern lads and lasses). You'd drive him mad to tell you the details of the trip. "What happened? What was the journey like? What do they eat? How was the Bovril?"

You would tell your friends at school about this epic journey and would vow that one day, you would all go up there in your minibus and conquer their fortress, liberate their fair dames and drink their pubs dry. Your brother would come back battered and bruised or fined and would listen to your mum and dad berate him for bringing disgrace on the family, and you would be told to stay away from that type: "It's poisoning the game." But you could not wait to stand on those terraces!

You became a teenager. You no longer needed big brother or Uncle Johnny. You had a milk round. You thought you had a few quid. You grew your hair long, had a moody tash and thought you could mix in with the big boys. You and your mates were invincible. You could tackle anyone. You stood at the fence by the away fans and called them w***ers and mugs. You were separated by a fence and the Old Bill, but thought you could rip it down and invade the away end on your white horse. You would say hi to the older members of the mob and they would laugh and snigger and mug you off, but you'd show them one day. You would be respected and would be part of their legion.

Then your world would come crashing down. You would encounter their top boys outside – remember the geezer you called w***er for ninety minutes? He remembered your face and made a beeline straight for you, fists and feet flying and frothing like a rabid dog, "Come 'ere, you little southern p**fter." You did your best but no match for Captain Caveman. The police would wade in, truncheons a-blazing and you would scuttle off, both frightened and elated, but bloody and sore. It was your first taste. Your mum and dad would be furious, what had they done so wrong? Where had they failed? Your older brother would snigger and make silly faces at you, but would also later commend you for your bravery. You were within an inch of your life, but didn't let it put you off and were the talk of the school Monday morning.

You would spend the next few seasons trying to be accepted by the crowd. Some of the nicer blokes might say 'allo but you would not fit in yet. You still had to earn your stripes, had merit points to score and especially had to prove yourself away. Going away in the 70s, 80s and 90s was not for the faint-hearted. No one liked you. There was no warm welcome. You were flash bastards who had repeatedly disrespected their homes, towns, women and team – you were not getting the red carpet treatment. It didn't matter if you were only going ten miles across town, you were entering their territory, their town and their world. You were not strutting about their manor giving it large. Their coppers hated you and were happy to wade in and were as up for it as their own fans were. These were the days when coppers were six feet tall, weighed two hundred pounds and looked like Vikings. They did not want you going home with a soft impression of their manor.

You would meet your mates at the mainline station, hoping the elders would allow you to stand in their region. Back then, you were even liable to get picked off by other teams travelling up or across and were fair game. A bonus and a nice start to the day. If you made it to the train, you were greeted by the football special. Now for those of us who were lucky (or unlucky) enough to remember this thing of beauty, you must know that at the time, us wonderfully well-behaved supporters were not thought of as so. British Rail were not going to lay on their best trains for us to wreck, piss and spill beer all over, and once they arrived at their destination, would get windows bricked in by our friends and comrades of the opposing team.

No, no, no. The football special was like a medieval battering ram that got you from A to B. It stank, had no upholstery and no creature comforts. There was no buffet service and the staff were drafted in especially for probably the worst shift imaginable. They had no sense of humour and all looked like prison guards from a Victorian era. You could spend up to seven hours there, only to arrive in a city or town waiting to take what remained of your spirit that was robbed up from the journey.

You would be herded to the ground, being abused and cajoled en route, and would be shown to their nicest seats, under cover from rain and wind, in their newly refurbished stand, where they'd serve hot cocoa and provide dry, warm blankets. Not! You would endure nearly two hours watching your team, wishing they would have stayed south of Watford. You would be wet and cold and would watch the same teenage fan call you all the w***ers under the sun and say disrespectful things about your sister. After this wonderful evening of light entertainment, you would be herded back to your "luxury carriage" and try to laugh and joke and booze your way through another six-odd hours of bone chilling, bone rattling torture, only to be dropped in the middle of town at four in the morning, wondering how the fudge you were going to get home.

You would get in wanting to take those soaked, cold clothes off and get into your pit, but you'd be met by your mum yelling at you, telling you how she was worried sick and that you weren't going to miss school again. Yet two weeks later (twenty-five milk rounds later), you were back heading in the same direction, warm welcome at the other end!

You'd now left school and felt you had earnt your stripes. You were loosely accepted by the elders. You might have been regarded as a good'un. You may have been afforded some manner of protection from away fans and you were now ready to step up.

I'm not strictly talking being a rucker. Many folk chose different paths throughout their journeys. Many were regarded as good, loyal supporters true to club and football, many aspired to the fashion part of the agenda. There were horses for courses, but the end game was always the same throughout this apprenticeship: you just wanted to meet friends with the same goals. You were the club's honoured fans and you were there for the right reasons. If you liked clothes, you wanted to be regarded as a dresser, or if you could have a ruck or were game, you were a thug. All the same, you were all united and were all doing your bit for a common cause.

You now had a job. You could spend money on clothes, travel, booze. You were fast becoming part of the accepted set, forming friendships with those you'd done your apprenticeship with and could now have a seat at the table. You just did not realise that the early years were the best, most exciting years. The pressures of life, future families and responsibilities would put a strain on this carnival ride. You were now at the table and had to maintain that seat.

Read on. I'll see you at the end, folks!

CD – Cardiff

I was definitely caught in no man's land. Born in 1972 to wonderful Irish Catholic parents who raised me and my three siblings in exactly the same way (discipline, love and affection in equal doses). We lived in a small south Wales town called Caldicot. Now considering its location to Newport, you would expect it to be County country but it was very much a City stronghold.

The "no man's land" part of my intro comes from the fact that due to Mum insisting I go to a Catholic school, it meant my comprehensive years were spent in Newport. This caused immediate issues as I stupidly let everyone know that my heart was blue and that their second-rate provincial town club was s**t. The consequence of that stupidity was having to fight my way through most lunchtimes over five years of senior school life. What that grounding in "enemy territory" gave me though, was an insight into the whole casual scene.

Newport always punched above their weight in footballing terms, but also in the sartorial stakes. I looked to key County lads for tips on what was what. The likes of Tutti, Lemmy Bullock, Adams, Billy Ingles and Farley were my clothing role models. I was awestruck by the Burberry shirts and golfing jackets, the cords, the Trimm Trabs, even the f**k off awful sovereign rings looked fantastic.

As per most lads of my age and academic ability, I left school at sixteen and got an apprenticeship within the construction industry. This newfound independence allowed me to purchase some late 80s/early 90s key essentials (Berghaus Pole jacket, Ball jeans, Saucony trainers). This gave me the misguided idea that I was now a "chap" and could follow my beloved Bluebirds the length and breadth of the UK.

Now here is where the second part of "no man's land" comes in. Certain sections of Cardiff lads knew where I had gone to school, and also knew that I was now friendly with certain County lads, who were considered "Top Lads". This in turn caused hostility at both City and Wales games. Essentially, I was considered an outsider by both groups. Now even though my first love was and will always be CCFC, due to family connections in London, I started to regularly travel east down the M4 and got a taste for ground hopping. Arsenal, Brentford, Charlton, even non-league matches caught my eye: Hayes, Sutton, Woking and Borehamwood. This venture opened my eyes to how different the South East lads dressed, with their attitude and swagger. It also gave me access to a musical and social scene that has stayed with me for the last thirty-something years.

Obviously, the casual scene has had direct connections to football-related disorder and most of us have had our run-ins over the years. Some good, some bad, some just ludicrously funny. What I can categorically state is that I never, ever hated anybody. The Saturday scene to me was a laugh, a giggle, time spent with great pals who thought, dressed and walked the same way. The whole peacock mentality that looking smart and feeling superior gave you. Although the waistline and hairline have changed considerably over the last thirty-two years, the desire to step out on match day knowing that you are dressed to within an inch of your life is still as important to me now as it was to the sixteen-year-old version of me back in '88.

Colin S – Motherwell

I was later to the casual scene than many. It was later in the 1980s and early 90s before I got heavily into the labels. I had been on the fringes at Motherwell for a while but coming from outside the town, it was a while before me and a few mates from our area were accepted. Motherwell lads were a huge influence on the house and modern soul scenes up here, probably more than any other Scottish casuals per head of population.

Motherwell is a small industrial town with a population of around 32,000, but we had decent numbers involved in football and clubbing up here from the outset really. Aberdeen were the first dressers up here, but Motherwell were next and miles ahead of the Glasgow clubs fashion-wise. Likewise, we were ahead of the game both soul and jazz funk-wise and definitely when house took over, Motherwell were at the forefront and we all bought into it.

By 1990–91, there were more Motherwell lads at club nights than football. I've been in clubs miles from the town with well over one hundred Saturday Service there. We very rarely saw violence at these events but it still occasionally kicked off, generally local feuds but there were a number of clashes with Hibs too. My then girlfriend, now wife, was hit in the face by broken glass when a stray pint glass launched by a prominent SS casual hit a wall next to us at a house night, in a nearby suburb of Motherwell. The place was trashed and a load of locals were hospitalised by Motherwell lads. My girl had to get the glass removed from her eye and was fortunate not to suffer much worse damage. That apart, we all embraced house and soul massively and still do to this day.

Neil L – Chelsea

My first memory of what came to be known as casual was probably fairly typical for my age group. We hit our teenage years as the 70s turned into the 80s typically sporting shaven heads or at least short crops, wearing DMs or Monkey boots, Tonic or Sta Press trousers, Waffle jumpers, Harrington's and Flight jackets.

I lived in Orpington which was technically one of London's leafy outer suburbs, but actually had quite an edge with some fairly nasty estates and a large traveller contingent who had a habit of making an appearance at any local pubs looking for a ruck at turning out time. My school was on the Ramsden Estate which was quite notorious at the time and produced the band Splodgenessabounds, as well as some renowned local Herbert's who kept the Old Bill busy in the town centre after dark. It was an angry time and the soundtrack fitted it perfectly as the late new wave stuff faded into a more political and aggressive style: The Specials, The Jam, early Madness, and Bad Manners with the likes of Inner London Violence.

However, change was in the air. A subtle one at first. As we got to the age of parties and discos, I noticed people's dress codes starting to change along with the music. Most people still wore their Flight jackets, but others had started to grow their hair and moved on to leather jackets, called box jackets and some others in an even cooler style called safari. Underneath, they wore golf jumpers with a lion on them which I soon found out were called Pringle (some had the name stitched underneath the lion). These were not in your traditional greys and navy blues. They were in pastel shades, yellows, light blues and even pinks, which got some stick from those who were still staunch skinheads. These guys were wearing grey or navy slacks to go with the jumpers, apparently called Farads, which had a little F tag on the back. And suddenly people were wearing trainers... not just any trainers, certainly not the type people previously wore for P.E. or indoor football. These were tennis trainers, Nike, Wimbledon, Blazer and Bruin, Adidas Forest Hill or Stan Smith and best of the lot: Diadora Borg Elite with gold or silver trim and the man himself's signature on it.

I was usually pretty fast on the uptake with these things and very quickly managed to cobble together a relevant outfit which consisted of grey Farahs, a roll neck from Gabicci in burgundy and a slate grey Lyle & Scott jumper which I'd purchased on a trip to a Sidcup golf shop by bus. That left the trainers to sort out. Luckily that year, our school had organised a trip to France which I had somehow persuaded my parents to pay for. Whilst most people were out buying flick knives, bangers and porno playing cards, I was hunting something else down... a pair of Stan Smiths which I had set my heart on.

The other thing I was spending my money on by that time was records... lots of them. I'd always had a broad taste courtesy of an uncle who had been a DJ and musician in a rock band. But I had got into something quite different: soul, jazz and funk which was having its golden era at the time. I had started listening to the pirate radio stations and hanging out at LPs, a record shop that got the latest import of 12-inch singles in. I once spent two months trying to track down a song I had heard on Radio Essex but misheard the song name and artist ("Dreamin'" by Greg Henderson, if you're interested).

It was the same with clothes. You couldn't just bowl down your local high street and pick it off a rack. It was hard to source and the old-fashioned men's shops mostly hadn't heard of it. It was the same at some barbers too: "A wedge you say?" When I first got mine cut in the style, I was asked, "Is your mum okay with that?" The whole thing was underground. It was youthful, vibrant and fresh, to use a word that came in a bit later with the sportswear craze.

That's the thing. Despite what we are told, there was not one casual look. There were several, often changing from month to month. Overall, the look that I had caught onto had been around for quite a while, which I learnt when I started to go to soul dos run by the pirate stations. Apart from lots of great new tunes, I soon discovered that the look had been about with the soul crowd first, and some of it, like Gabicci and Farahs, had come from the black lads who had brought it from the reggae parties to the soul all dayers.

My previously treasured Lyle & Scott was sold to a kid at school who was a bit slow on the uptake (he did support Charlton after all) which I used to fund a Jaeger jumper I'd tracked down in Army and Navy, Victoria Street. By this time, I was wearing an Adidas cagoule to school with the red lining and a pair of Farahs, with matching jumper. The Adidas item had come from football, specifically a trip to Stamford Bridge when I'd noticed half of the West Stand benches wearing one. Like many Londoners, I was both into football and the soul boy thing. Actually, the transformation from an army of green and blue Flight jacketed skins, to floppy-haired casuals wasn't instant at Chelsea. But given the amount of clued-up West London lads about, some crossover was there early on. There's a photo of a very well-known Chelsea legend wearing a golf jumper, trainers and Adidas T-shirt leading a mob towards White Hart Lane in '77/'78 for instance. Not that I could claim that. I was still in snorkel parka and flares, sitting in the West Stand from 1976–80.

The sportswear craze was suddenly huge in '82/'83 and one lad at school was somehow able to turn up in full Tacchini or Ellesse tracksuits every day. I'm still not sure how. In fact, that is the only time I saw anyone wear a full suit despite what Nick Love seems to remember. The tennis gear look almost certainly did come down from the Scousers, with the exception of Lacoste which was already about. It was a cracking look at the time but didn't hang around as the smarter and more expensive labels were coming in. Burberry, Aquascutum, Balmain, Nani Bon, Armani etc. all took off, and only the younger kids still wore tennis gear, which was crap as I loved my Ellesse bucket hat at the time. The whole point was that it was about being fresh and exciting and new, looking forward not backwards like the mods, teds and skins. In came Paninaro, Surf T-shirts, paisley, slicked-back hair, pointy collars, checked shirts and more.

The media never cottoned on to it. By the time they got a sniff, it was long gone. If you trawl through YouTube, you might find one short clip of 80s kids from West London with Stuarts in it. The rest is regurgitated stuff made much later. Most of it was nonsense, trying to link the cause with Britpop or something else it had no connection with.

As with anything, it finally came to an end, ironically killed off by a culture spurred on by house music and a complete opposite of what casual was about... baggy, shapeless gear and Clarks Wallabies of all things. Of course, there have been revivals, and when eBay started up, I think I rebought quite a lot of old favourites, but a Fila BJ doesn't look great on a middle-aged man. In fact, what track top does? Even football managers hide their guts with a puffer jacket. So, like the original casual, I moved on and found new labels, with the occasional nod to the past if I can find something that actually looks okay. If I get nostalgic, I can always check out old photos. There's one of me at Selhurst in 1983 in front of a Chelsea Union Jack wearing a diamond Pringle for instance. If only I hadn't scratched my head at that very moment, you'd be able to see my face.

On New Year's Day '89, I went to Oxford away, dressed in a suede-look bomber jacket, black M&S wool jumper, Levi 501s and boat shoes. I couldn't get into the packed away end so we merged into the queue for the home end, as you did. I was just about to walk towards the turnstile when a copper yells, "Oi you! You're not coming in." When I asked why, he said, "You look too much like a Londoner." Perhaps you never lose it...

Richard P – Rotherham

From a small northern town, Rotherham, I started going to Millmoor in 1974 with my dad, and the odd away game too. I wasn't really interested in music until the last few years at comp, when I was mainly into The Jam, The Specials and then the New Romantic movement kicked in. I never wore the clothes or the hair style associated with them. I still had the Bruce Foxton spike. My best mate, a year older than me, started to wear Pringle and Lyle & Scott. Still being at school, I was wearing Fred Perry's from the local sport shops.

On leaving school, I did my first-year apprenticeship in Sheffield. By this time, I'd ventured into bleached frayed jeans, Puma G Vilas trainers, the turquoise Patrick cagoule and Fila tracksuit top finished with a few sprays of 1881 Cerruti. We then realised we were a good few months behind the big city boys. The Sheffield United lads were one step ahead, wearing Burberry,

Aquascutum, Gee 2; a fashion that would catch on a few months later in our town. Music-wise, I was into New Order. I went to see them a few times with an older pal who was a Blade. We would regularly go on shopping jaunts to Manchester, straight off the train at Piccadilly and into Hurleys. We were like a couple of dogs with two knobs. We didn't know what to look at next. It was Aladdin's cave. Then onto the underground market. The Manc girls in their snorkel parkas looked so cool, with their bob haircuts, bleached jeans and trainers.

On a few holidays abroad, we accidentally met up with likeminded youths from Hull and Liverpool. We all seemed to like the same music and wore similar clobber. At the time, The House Martins had burst onto the scene. In the mid to late 80s, the Madchester Scene was on the horizon. I saw The Happy Mondays as back up for New Order at the NEC. We were Armanied up, nice Ball and Adidas. A big part of the crowd were wearing the baggy jeans and oversized sweatshirts. I continued to love the Manchester music: Inspiral Carpets, The Stone Roses, The Charlatans.

Then the football lads' world was ripped apart as the rave scene kicked in during the late 80s and early 90s. We went from between thirty and sixty lads on a good day to about a dozen or so who regularly travelled up and down the country watching Rotherham, whilst the lost lads were popping pills and dancing in fields and warehouses up and down the land. We had rivalries with local sides in the bottom two divisions.

In the early 2000s, we made the promised land of the Championship. Our group got bigger, the same as the other clubs. The higher you got, the bigger the opposition. I'd been watching England regularly at home since the mid-80s and started going away in the early 2000s. I went from being in a mob of maximum seventy likeminded lads to a crowd of several. It was a massive buzz. I didn't miss an England away game for a few years.

Clothes-wise, these days I seem to have gone nearly full circle: Lois cords, Gabicci, Trojan, Art Gallery, with a few newish labels, like Nemen, Battenwear and the reliable class Paul&Shark.

Respect to all the lads from all over the land that were involved. Our generation were the instigators for today's youth.

Johnny S – Queens Park Rangers

My journey into casual started in '82 or '83. Growing up in Sutton in the suburbs of South London, the look was everywhere. We'd all been diddy mods, but were too young for the mod revival. Our time was yet to come.

I'd never heard the term "casual". It wasn't a term we used. The lads with the burgundy lowlights or blond highlights in their wedge haircuts, we knew as "jazz funkers". I can only speak about my experiences, and for me, the look never came from football. It just so happened the lads that went to the match were mainly casuals, a bit like skinheads in the late 60s. Their look didn't come from the terraces, but it did go hand in hand with football and agg at the match.

For me, our look was a mix of West Indian Stixman and that brash South London spivvy/wide boy/black cab driver look. Taking the look in no small part from the soul boys too. It certainly wasn't coming from

Liverpool. It was proper working-class street style. It seemed like everyone wore the look in London, not just the chaps at football. You didn't have to be a hooligan or even go to matches, and the local girls wore the look too, with their Burberry trench coats and Lady Diana flicks. One thing I noticed going to watch my team, QPR, was that there it seemed everyone was a casual, even older blokes dressed in Pringles and Farahs with crocodile skin loafers etc. It crossed the race boundaries too, with black lads carrying off the look with some panache, with their Aquascutum and deerstalker hats. For the northerners, it was only their chaps who dressed. It certainly didn't seem mainstream like it was down here.

Talking about QPR, it probably helped having Stuarts on the Uxbridge Road. It's potentially a biased recollection but I always felt we had some of the best dressed lads around, maybe second only to Arsenal. They always seemed to be ahead on the style front. So, my early look would be hair in a wedge, then it was grown longer at the back, flicked at the front and shorter at the sides. It ended up getting well past collar length. There was a craze one summer for hair dye and I even had it permed at one point! It came to about '86 when I had it all cut off and gelled back. It probably stayed that way for a couple of years until acid house reared its head. Then there was a period of frantic hair growing, starting with a middle parting, then curtains and ending with a long ponytail that went way down past my shoulders.

Now for the clothes. You have to bear in mind that in the early 80s, I was a young teenager, so anything I mention is what I could afford at the time. My working-class parents didn't understand the whole label thing, especially my old man. He thought wearing deodorant was for p**fs (as he would say) so seeing his only son with gold earrings, dyed hair and a pink Burberry scarf was incomprehensible. I'm listing things in the order from the early 80s to about 1990. I started with Gabicci knitwear, then V-neck diamond Pringles, Lyle & Scotts or crew neck Robe di Kappa lambswool jumpers. By the mid-80s, Armani, but that was proper expensive, going into brands like Chevignon and Naf Naf by the late 80s. Trousers were Farahs, light grey for school and burgundy for football, Lois – faded with frayed bottoms and inch cuts on the seams so they'd hang over your trainers. I had Lois jumbo cords in loads of different shades but electric blue was my favourite. I even had a pair in a bright lemon shade, which caused me no end of grief, getting picked out in the away end of White Hart Lane, then running the gauntlet afterwards on the Seven Sisters Road. Lois gave way to Pepe jeans and C17s, with the latter still being worn right the way into the acid house scene. Adidas Gazelles and Stan Smiths were always my favourite shoes, but Nike Wimbledon were massive too, as were Diadora Borg Elites and Apollo boots, which were big round my way. Kickers too, which eventually gave way to Wallabies and Fila boots.

Fashion moved really quickly and what was acceptable one month was out the next. A lot of clothes were sold on to younger kids who couldn't afford the latest gear and a lot of taxing went on. If you were in another manor on your own, you had to be very careful leaving a shop, especially with that shop's bag, because the local casuals would happily relieve you of your latest purchase. In a similar manner, if you were from outside our area and you left Budwals in Croydon, or Troubadour in Sutton, you might not have made it home with your gear. So, the look went from Stixman, funkers, through to the smart golfer-type getting into the baggier casual look of the late 80s raver. There were many other labels and trends I've missed here. These are just things that stand out to me in my memory.

For us on the music scene, electro and early hip-hop was the order of the day. I still loved The Jam, and The Style Council really caught the mood. Soul and funk were big too, think of "I Found Lovin'" by The Fatback Band or "You're the One for Me" by D Train etc. When house music came out, that changed everything: fashion, drugs, night time activities!

One thing I've got to say was the whole Madchester thing passed us by. That was for scruffy northerners and students in our opinion (no offence). We were strictly house and acid at the time. After the house scene ended, I reverted back to more of my mod look. I still go to Rangers and look back at the 80s casual times with very fond memories.

Carpy – West Ham

I was born and bred in Chelmsford so didn't really have any affinity with the East End of London or West Ham. My dad was born on Kings Road, Chelsea and Mum in deepest, darkest rural Essex at Leaden Roding. Dad took me to watch Chelmsford City as a five-year-old and that's where my love of football started. They regularly had crowds of 3000 or 4000 in those days. My real passion for West Ham began simply because of the secondary school I went to: Rainsford Comprehensive. There were many, many older lads there that supported them and that's how I got into it.

Wayne Stiles (who still goes home and away) took me to my first game, versus Coventry, just before the FA Cup final in 1975. If my memory serves me well, it was the same day Spurs played Chelsea at White Hart Lane and it kicked off on the pitch and around the ground. We saw a load of them fighting at Liverpool Street station, and me being a naïve fourteen-year-old, wanted to go and have a look at what was going on... with my West Ham scarf on, which wasn't a good idea.

The next season, I started to go regularly (although Mum wouldn't let me go to the Man U game as they had regularly been causing trouble the previous season, but I think we all know what happened at that game). A lot of my mates now are ones that I met on the train or at Chelmsford station. One person in particular, Bob Mayer, introduced me to loads more at West Ham who are still friends to this day.

So, forty-five years on, and I'm still going. The football hasn't got any better. We're in a new ground which will never be a patch on the Boleyn. There's been some good times and some bad times, but one thing has been constant, and that's my mates and the characters I've met.

Magz – Stockport

Any lad that served their time on the football terraces of Britain can spot another lad a mile off. It's not just the clobber but also the stance, the confidence, the attitude; somehow projecting a wry smile at the pointlessness of being in this room with lesser mortals, or at least "normals" who don't know the score.

This only works, of course, until you have one too many at the works do and ask the chap in the nice CP who he follows. You should have known not to go on when you had to explain that you were talking about football. Then when he responds with a timid "Burnley", it probably isn't wise to smirk and point out what a bunch of inbred, scruffy c**ts they were (and probably still are) and what a surprise it is that CP is now available in Home Bargains. It's only when he displays complete confusion and stammers that his brother gave him the coat, that he doesn't know anything about "getting done" at the Waldorf in Manchester in the 90s as he's only held a season ticket with his boy (who goes to Lancaster Grammar, by the way) since they got to the Premier League, that you realise your radar isn't as finely tuned as it used to be! Nor does it help that he's the project manager for Network Rail and that there might be a difficult conversation in the office come Monday morning.

The night is saved, of course, when you bump into the lad who does the fit outs at the depot and he's sporting a vintage Stoney that was packed into his overnight bag. Turns out he's an old Blade and you once had him running for cover down a grassy slope near the station in Sheffield. You don't have time to bask in the glory before you both realise he was there the night you got "tuned in" outside a Sheffield city centre pub. As you can imagine, old battles are then re-fought, common friends and enemies identified, clothes and music thoroughly discussed and another daft friendship forged.

I'm not a football violence bore, by the way. In fact, I hardly ever mention it, but I can't take my ale these days and therefore tend to take myself away from the situation instead. Don't listen to my close mates when they tell you I could never take my beer and would fall asleep by six o'clock. That takes me back, all the way to The Swan, our pub from the late 80s and all through the 90s. The table was s**t, which goes some way to explaining my shortcomings as a pool player, but the location was all important. When we started drinking in The Swan, we were just lads, the "younger lot" with our own little roll call of disparate youth. The old campaigners, at least into their twenties by then, started off in The Unity on the other side of the station and worked their way up to Edgeley via The Armoury (next door to us), then The Grapes and on to any one of the six other pubs then in existence on Castle Street. You might wonder why I'm starting to write a historical piece for CAMRA but I assure you I'm not (I'll leave that to my mate Olly). I'm just trying to set the scene.

We had chosen The Swan as our base for a couple of reasons. Firstly, it was down on its luck since getting smashed up in 1984 in an FA Cup tie against Telford (windows that had been in place for 200 years disappearing in the process) and as the regulars had stopped going in, we were welcomed as customers. Secondly, and more Importantly, sitting on the roundabout between Greek Street and Castle Street, it covered three of the four main approaches to Edgeley Park and any away fan not coming by coach or car would walk close by it, or at least within a couple of streets. From The Swan, we could stroll down to The Bluebell, directly opposite the station approach, or check The Church, The Greyhound or The Old Vic in the surrounding streets (more f'in pubs).

Clashing with the opposition in the days before mobile phones generally relied on chance meetings, but you could narrow those odds by being switched on and we were hungry for such encounters. Some of the older lot would get pissed off with us at times because we'd kick it off with any football lads we came across and this would sometimes bring unwanted attention from the coppers before the "main lot" from the opposition had arrived. It's an old, old story though, and I remember getting upset with young lads years later when they were acting up before we'd got to where we needed to be, but they were only being us at a similar age.

I should tell you at this stage that all Stockport County lads have a bit of a chip on their shoulder. I'm not frightened to admit it and in fact I'm f****ng proud of it because it makes us what we are. There are similar stories out there, but first and foremost we're football fans and care deeply about our club. Following a Championship season in the late 60s, Stockport through the 70s and 80s served up more than two decades of mediocrity and under-achievement. On four occasions, we were re-elected to the football league by the skin of our teeth. These hardships created a small but fiercely loyal following with an "us against them" attitude and a thick skin to shield against the derision of neighbours and work colleagues who had deserted their hometown club for bragging rights amongst the elite.

Then came the 90s. A decade of unrivalled success on the pitch (and some serious fun and games off it). Bearing in mind this abrupt change in our footballing fortunes, perhaps we would have been justified in thinking our long-time detractors would have slapped us on the back, shaken our hand and said, "Well done!" In fact, much of our success was either ignored, in the case of local and national media, or greeted with bitterness and spite, especially from fans of neighbouring clubs who seemed to believe that our position as anything other than a music hall joke was an outrage. That's the reason we celebrated hard, rubbed people's noses in it and probably shouted a bit too loudly at the time. Thus, we must also take some of the credit for their enjoyment during our subsequent decline.

For the lads, there was a similar trajectory off the pitch as well. We had our fair share of "reversals" home and away, but whenever we got one over on the big boys like Birmingham, West Brom, Everton, Liverpool, Stoke, Sheffield Wednesday... (you get the picture) they'd either pretend it didn't happen or fabricate a story about a Man City firm being there, which if you know anything about us at all is pure fantasy. I'm not complaining about these things though because "those who know, know". It certainly helped to push us closer together, make us a tight unit and a force to be reckoned with on our day.

My involvement with County evolved from hanging out in Stockport town centre on a Saturday morning in the early 80s. Me and my mate Dennis lived and went to school outside Stockport but were drawn in by a burgeoning, though short-lived, break-dancing scene. Dennis was a pretty decent body-popper for a fifteen-year-old and I was a pretty s**t break-dancer for any age. It's cringeworthy now remembering lads from different areas of Stockport battling it out on a piece of old lino in the precinct. It was less "Break Dance - Electric Boogie" and more "B-Boys Beware", but it was a step on the path to somewhere, although certainly not to stardom. There was a crossover with the casual scene and much of the sports gear found its way from the lino to the terraces, with Adidas, New York and First tops, Kappa coats and Kangol hats amongst them. Me and Dennis were just graduating from the earlier "Perry boy" look, with the flick (or wedge) haircut, bleached jeans and sports top, giving way to longer hair at the back with streaks and more expensive knitwear.

It was at this time, at least in our area, that the "top boy" look emerged, which seemed to be marked by a tight perm on the top and back of the head. Sadly, often accompanied by a dodgy 'tash, but thankfully this flourish was short-lived and not adopted by most in our particular scene. On Saturdays, we also had a habit of going to the pool hall by the bus station, which had an arcade and, while you could rent a table for pennies, it cost a fortune in ten pence pieces to keep the light on. Just in case you had any complaints, there were a couple of well-known lads on the door, who would be more than happy to help you leave through the still-closed door. It was also infamous for naïve kids getting preyed on by more streetwise or harder lads, so you had to keep your wits about you and watch who you chatted to. We got to know a few lads by sight and one such Saturday, a well-dressed couple of lads from the Heaton Chapel part of town asked us if we were going up to the match. I hadn't shown much affinity for watching football outside Match of the Day and the FA Cup final up until then, but I loved the game and having heard the jokes about Stockport County at school I was intrigued as to how bad it could be.

The match turned out to be one of the worst games I had ever seen and football-wise seemed to confirm the bleakness of life at Edgeley Park, but I was fascinated. In a crowd of around 2000 was a raucous group of a hundred or so who never stopped making noise throughout a dismal one-all draw. They stood under the roof on the Popular Side in the first half then moved round onto the open Railway End in the second, when County were playing towards it. Instinctively, I joined the choir in the second half and started to sing along, immersing myself in it, with the chilly breeze blowing down my neck off the peaks and across the railway yard behind and the dank autumn smells mingling with savoury aromas from burgers, baked potatoes and pies. Cigarette smoke lingered in the air as the feeble floodlights attempted to spotlight the dreary performance on the pitch. Sounds pretty grim, doesn't it? But I was hooked!

Now, before I drift further into this reminiscence, which is much more spiritual and atmospheric in the re-telling than the reality at the time, I can tell you that was probably the last time I joined the choir for anything like forty-five minutes (although I've been known to have a cheeky sing now and then since), because late in the proceedings I noticed another group. Our two mates from the pool hall were standing with a group of about thirty lads, off to one side chatting and smoking; sometimes clapping with the chants but otherwise aloof. All of these lads were smartly dressed, with decent sports gear, a couple of very smart patchwork leathers, short leather jackets, straight leg jeans and trainers; hands in pockets, elbows out, cocky and proud. It was hard to know what they were so "cocky and proud" about on a cold October evening in Stockport, but at the time I thought they looked the business. And so, it commenced.

Me and Dennis started hanging around the fringes of these lads and even snatching a brief word or two with the older lot. The odd home game turned into every home game, bricking it the first time the opposition showed up unexpectedly and you had to get involved. Then getting asked for the first time to meet up for the train to a local game or making up the numbers on the coaches or in the back of a van; sometimes we got lucky enough to get a real seat in a minibus. Those were days when we lived for the Saturday afternoon or the Friday night. When you rarely had time to finish that bag of chips from the Union Chippy because Bolton, Blackpool or Preston had just turned up. Or the joy of the landlord serving you a pint in The Grapes, as long as you stood in the pool room where the coppers couldn't see you. Happy days and happy nights before mobile phones, CCTV, arranged meets and paranoia about police infiltration.

The education in clobber continued apace with Farah trousers, Pringle jumpers and Lyle & Scott fast appearing and disappearing. Paisley shirts (Fiorucci and the like) were adopted after a trip to London by a couple of us, when the golf gear was getting a bit dated and the eternal search continued for names which no one else was wearing, but somebody somewhere undoubtedly was. Personally, I loved the Lee semi-flared cords (pincord rather than jumbo) sported by some northern firms, going perfectly with a pair of Gazelles and like kryptonite to most of our London-based friends. They looked perfect with a dark Lacoste polo. The quest for the correct cloth was supported by Gansgear and later Zico in Stockport, while frequent forays into Manchester to Hurleys, Flannels, Kendals and their ilk were often fruitful. With Armani and Aquascutum on King Street, the wish list just got longer. I didn't rob any of my gear, by the way. Which isn't the start of some virtuous commentary, but only because since being caught stealing a Twix at eight years old in my local newsagent, I knew I was s**t at it and would get a beam on if I even thought about it. So, I was limited to buying and ordering second hand gear off others or digging into my own limited funds, sometimes reckless in the choice of purchase, to obtain something unique and get ahead of the game. Although often with very mixed success.

I've noticed that some people keep trying to make casual fashion "linear" in respect of "this happened then, and then that" in order to say they were first with something. But, it's simply not true. The truth is the fashions bounced back and forth and lads would take home what they'd liked on an away trip (often after ridiculing the lad wearing it) and reject the rest. Different firms found different clobber acceptable at different times and the looks evolved because of it. Although I'm sure it's true that Cardiff were wearing Stone Island in 1972 and it was a Scouser called Peter Storm who invented the cagoule.

For me, as for most lads, music was an influence throughout, but I didn't stick to any particular genre. The first records I bought were Madness, Ultravox and OMD. I listened disinterestedly to the lads at school when we were about twelve and they would argue which band was mod and which ska. I loved The Specials, The Beat, The Jam and The Who, but I drew a line at agreeing The Police were mods just because Sting wore a Who T-shirt in a video. Adam and the Ants might have had an influence, but I would generally admit to listening to all the cool bands while pretending not to like Duran Duran and keeping my hip-hop collection under wraps. My brother liked Simple Minds and U2 which rubbed off enough for me to go and see U2 in an ace concert in 1984, by which I've measured all other live performances since. I went off them in the 90s when they got too clever. Through my brother, I also got into a band called The Chameleons, from Middleton in Manchester, who were very successful at the indie underground level and were one of the bands who I believe formed the basis of what would come later in Manchester and the north west. This also informed my love of live music at all venues from pub to arena and, to this day, anyone who's brave enough to step on a live stage with a microphone or instrument has my full respect.

My days of innocence, of eating chips on the fringes of a row, of toying with terrace life would come to a brutal, jarring halt in an incident after an away match was called off in Rochdale. It's not the time or the place to go too deeply into it now, but following that day, I was a much darker soul when it came to a scrap at the football and I recognise now where it started. It's possibly the only incident of its kind that I've never forgiven and perhaps I'm being hypocritical after some of the things I did later. But then I've never sung a song about nearly stabbing kids to death. It still stirs me to anger.

The year after the Rochdale incident, August 1986 to be exact, I joined the armed forces. After which, through determination and some bad behaviour on my part, I managed to continue my appearances on the football terraces. However, my service would limit my chances to go each week and severely dent my ability to follow the national team home and away for the next nine years. But then again, where there's a will, there's a way!

Ady C – West Ham

I am fifty-four years old and now live in Lowestoft, Suffolk. I was born in Croydon in 1965. My mum was from Croydon and my dad was from Lambeth, so I've got South London blood in my veins but have always supported my beloved West Ham. Trevor Brooking was my idol so the choice was made to follow the Hammers.

My first game was in 1979 and I stood on the North Bank at Upton Park. I quickly noticed the strong characters around the ground and in the local pubs. After about a year, I had made some lifelong friends, many from the train travelling down from Norfolk, Suffolk and Essex.

By the early 80s, I was completely hooked, going to every game home and away. We had our own little firm all under the ICF banner with lads from Essex, Suffolk, East, West and North London, Wales and Swindon. We called ourselves the Upping Firm. We were all quite young and had many friends in the U5s, as well as the older lot. Someone once said if you could bottle the buzz we all got from football, it would be better than any drug. I loved the fashion and music. I was into jazz funk and soul. Everything in my life revolved around going to football. I even blew an old girlfriend out so I could go to Watford away, and that wasn't a big game for us back then. I don't think the younger lot these days know how dangerous it was back then. Travelling on the Underground, you never knew who you would bump into. Our haunt was Liverpool Street, so there was always plenty of West Ham about; but West Ham lads travelling across from West London etc. took their life in their hands.

I did get into the rave scene in 1988 and did the warehouse promoting and Ibiza thing, but by the mid-90s, I'd had enough of partying. It had also changed as well as the football scene. I met a girl and had a son who, by the way, is West Ham. He had no choice. I had worked on the ship yards and when they closed, I went to work offshore on the oil rigs so spent a lot of time away working. I did stay away from football for a few years but once my son was older, I got back in touch with everyone again and it's like we have never been away. I know we were all a bit naughty back in the day but the friendships we have all made are very special and will never be broken. I still get the same buzz travelling down to East London as I did all those years ago, as they say, "West Ham till we die."

Brian H – Portsmouth

It all started for me by going to football in the late 70s. I used to stand in the Fratton end jumping up and down and throwing the odd toilet roll. In '79, I left school just as two-tone started. Around about this time, I remember watching the Havelock Skins steaming into the Swindon mob at the Milton End, with the chants of "Pompey Aggro Hello" ringing in my ears. I was hooked so I became a skin. Shirt King was the main shop in Pompey to buy your clothes from. Although there were other mobs in Pompey, I would say the Havelock Skins were the main boys. They took their name from a pub they went to called The Havelock in Landport, a council estate in the middle of Portsmouth.

From Skinhead to Casual

Pompey had gained promotion to the old third division in 1980. The game that was on everyone's mind was Millwall. We first played them just after Christmas. Every loon it seemed from Pompey went on a special train. 'Wall didn't disappoint, with fighting before, during and after the game. This was the start of what would become a big rivalry between us and them. We had to wait until April of '81 for the home fixture. There was the usual trouble but what stood out that day was the way Millwall was dressed: Slazenger jumpers and Adidas kicks. I remember this because of some Millwall chap calling us scruffy, the majority of us still being skins. Crossover 1981.

The Casual Scene

By the 1982/83 season, the casual scene had exploded down here: everywhere around you saw Pringle jumpers from the local golf shops, Lois jeans and cords from a shop called Hellrazor in Pompey's city centre, also a shop in Fareham called Ski Sun for Fila/Sergio Taccini tracksuit tops. We took an odd trip to Lillywhites in

London for trainers and Stuart's at Shepherd's Bush where you had to have your wits about you or you could end up losing your new purchase. Later on, it was Nik Naks in Soho and Cecil Gee. We also used to pop up the road to Southampton (scum) for Patrick cagoules and later the Benetton shop.

The 6.57 Crew

I think most people know where the name came from. It was from the first train out of Portsmouth and Southsea train station to London Waterloo. In 1983, The Face magazine ran an article on the football casual and an interview with a Millwall geezer about dressing casual. This prompted a lad to write a letter stating this was not just a London thing and that Pompey have some snappy dressers. He signed it: The 6.57 Crew. The rest is history.

Over the years, Pompey pulled some strokes, going into Millwall and Birmingham seats suited and booted, pretending to go to a wedding at Cardiff, taking push bikes to Cambridge just for a laugh. That's just mentioning a few.

I think it's in order to mention the general election in '87 when one of the lads would run for Parliament under the 657 banner. That lad was the late Docker Hughes and managed to get 455 votes, as far as I'm aware no other football firm has ever done this.

Bringing this to an end, I still love my clothes. I can't see myself dressing any other way. But now I'd rather meet up with likeminded lads from other teams and have a pint and a chat about the old times. Play up, Pompey!

Derek C – Brighton

You've got to look the bollocks, right? So, our first away game on a Saturday actually starts the day before with a trip to the Lanes in Brighton. You get a new Fila roll neck, Pringle argyle sweater, don't need new jeans, and you're gonna wear your Nike Wimbledons. So, it's Saturday morning, up with the lark, clobber on, quick glance in the mirror. Yep, you're looking the dogs. You meet the lads down the railway station, making sure someone has remembered to bring the ghetto blaster, as there's nothing better than blasting out The Buzzcocks, The Clash and The Jam as we supped our warm Stellas.

On arrival, you can hear our lads singing at the pub we have taken over, nothing better than meeting up and seeing all your mates dressed in their finest. The floor is awash with Adidas, Nike and Puma and only getting arsey when someone bumps into you and half a pint goes straight down your faded jeans and splashes your new Gazelles. Outside for a quick puff (nothing better than showing off your clobber to all and sundry). Football's over, now into town and a few clubs. It's strange how we roll in, grab a pint and focus on what the mushes are wearing. "Where did you get that jumper from?" someone asks me. "Down the Lanes in Brighton," I say, "I'm going Friday if you fancy a day out, a few beers, and buy some more clobber." Those were the days!

Nikki P – Heart of Midlothian

I was born in 1967, in Edinburgh. I went through high school in the 80s. This was a hard time as we had no real belonging in society, too young to get into the pubs and clubs, and too cool for youth clubs. My brothers supported Heart of Midlothian Football Club, so naturally I followed them to the games, unaccompanied by adults, who were unaware where we were all day, and not that interested as long as we got home for tea. We jumped the barriers at stadiums, climbed fences, hung out of mates' windows to watch the home games, or even more interesting, the skinheads fighting in the Shed; the pitch invasions and the sheer excitement driven by a territorial anger on their faces. It was always a buzz, something to belong too. In Edinburgh, you were either Hearts or Hibs. It was always banter at school with nothing too serious. Then came "away days".

Now, this is where I feel for me things changed, probably around 1984. We went to every game and stood in the "Shed". It was incredible just people watching, and the tension was palpable. There were no seating areas in the Shed. It was the corner of the home stand and full of skinheads. It had a dangerous feel but with that came an excitement, adrenaline, an addiction to the buzz. Plus, you know everyone in the ground was one team, a mob. I stood at the fence beside the away end with my mate, a small crowd of Hearts stood beside us, and none had scarfs on. I knew them by face but not by name. One said, "We are CSF. Do you girls want to stand with us?" And so, it all began. We travelled the country, although not that involved with physical violence, we were lookouts. We gave an alibi when the police came. Police tended not to arrest the guys that were with a girl. I am still friends with those same people now. We still look out for each other. There were only about five girls at this time, three of us are all still close today. The lads were all our mates and brothers. We grew up together.

It was 1985/86, we had just left school. Hearts were playing away. I remember the clothes, the trainers, the tension as the train pulled into Dundee, the usual shouts of "Nobody run!" It was carnage. Going to either of the big Glasgow games was a massive adrenaline rush, even as the train approached Queen Street

271

station. Sometimes the girls would head through first and go into a bar on George Square. We could watch where the opposition were waiting and give our lot the heads up. Most Scottish mobs could be identified with the different trends. We always felt top notch because, after all, we were from the capital. Now, the other mobs all had girls, but Hearts lads looked after us.

It's hard to put into words why I loved it. Going to football was a way of life for us back then. That feeling is still there now. There wasn't much else for us to do back then. I did get into some tricky situations, and I do have a criminal record because of this but I'm not ashamed. It's made me who I am. The people I met throughout Scotland and England I still class as friends today. Loyal good people who support each other still to this today.

Paul B – Tottenham

I was born in '62, in Hammersmith. My dad took me to Fulham, but one Saturday he said, "Come on, son, we're going to Spurs versus Chelsea." This was 1975. The first time I saw trouble at a scale. That afternoon, Chelsea were chased onto the pitch. After the game, anyone thought to be Chelsea meant to take a bad kicking. The next game was Leeds at home. He took me to that as well. I was hooked.

In the early 80s, everyone had their Fila, Pringles, Nike Wimbledons, but no mobile phones. We had train travel on the football specials, then the 125s. This time we went everywhere, very dangerous times in those days. I can remember going to King's Cross or Euston most Saturday nights to see if anyone was there, and nine times out of ten there was. Taxing became a bad part of the scene. I remember going to Swank, Nic Naks and Lillywhites – what a shop that was. I remember being in Luton Arndale Centre one Saturday and a fella came up to me and said, "Where did you get your Trimm Trabs? Can I try them on?" Not a chance.

Then the rave scene came about. We used to go to King's Cross and Dalston for the warehouse things. After a while, you used to see loads of lads from other teams just chatting and getting on. I dropped out after that for about ten years, then I got the bug again and started going Spurs again up until recently. Oh, what days we had.

Joe M – Everton

I was a child of the 60s who grew up in an area of Liverpool called Kirkdale. One of five kids (the baby), but more importantly, I was brought up in an Everton family. I first started going to the games with my dad and his mate, Peter Butcher. My first away match was in the 1969/70 season. We never missed a home or away game whilst I was growing up. I was a bit spoilt going the match, as I always had boss seats and went in boss cars, Rolls Royce, Mercedes, Jags, which was boss. But I was too young to realise what I was in, so no chance of bragging.

My dad was a grafter all his life, and was certainly part of a large firm in Liverpool, and was a known face in the city. Throughout my childhood, the police coming to the house was nothing new. Seeing my dad on Granada news, Cat A, going to all the major jails in the country to visit him, was just a normal thing for me and the rest of the family. Meeting known gangsters

IT'S ALL ABOUT THE BUZZ

like Frankie Frasier and Timmy Newnan was nothing. It was that regular, that when they were both in Wakefield, Frank's sister Eve, would come down the day before and stay overnight in my mum's, so she could come with us to see them.

My dad got me my first season ticket in the main stand (row A, seat number seven), in 1971 and to this day I can still see my old seat, and the woman who sat by me then, now sits behind me in 2020. Looking back on what I witnessed at the Millwall game in 1973, it was a scary place to be for a ten-year-old, even with my aunties sitting behind me. I have to give it to Millwall. They had the bottle to go in the Street End, but it backfired major league for them, with so many getting stabbed and battered. It was a brawl, still vivid in my memory forty-six years later, and yet I can't remember what I did last week.

By the time my dad got jail for armed robbery in '79, I was going to the games with my mates, really getting into the football scene, but very much on the peripheries of the Everton firm. We were close enough through drinking in town to know them and get on with them. At that time in my life, Liverpool was a brilliant city to grow up in, especially for the music and for me being an Everton fan.

By the time I was seventeen (in 1980), I was becoming more and more involved with Everton's firm, and enjoying the experiences of going away with the blues, and even more importantly, meeting firms coming into Liverpool. The bar to be in was Star & Garter, which at the time was the meeting place for the ordinaries coming into the city via Lime Street. We had some great scraps with various teams coming out of the side entrance of Lime Street, with the police (who I will say were the hardest bizzies on the planet) trying desperately hard to separate lads who wanted to dance in the street.

The 80s were great for loads of firms, coming of age with new heads coming into the firms, taking over from the lads in the 60s and 70s. I always loved meeting West Ham, Arsenal and Spurs, but especially Man U, as that was at the height of the Munich period, where at every opportunity, we would fight with them. They had a boss firm (more numbers than any other firm – mainly Cockney Reds). But life wasn't just about football violence, it was about going out with the lads and waiting for excitement.

To this day, nothing has changed. Fifty-seven, but eighteen in my head. To put it simply, the casual movement defined me as a person: loyal, won't back off and will never leave a mate. Not a bad thing to live your life by.

Ali – Celtic

Don't Stop the Dance – Roxy Music

The match was my first day out against Aberdeen. I had been at a few games with the crew on the lead up to this. I remember seeing calling cards going about stating: "Congratulations, you just have met the Celtic Soccer Trendies." Although the mob were chanting "Celtic Soccer Crew", so we seemed to have settled on CSC.

I got to know faces from the terraces over time. They told us we were occupying the bottom of the main stand at Celtic Park next to the old Rangers end (the away end) so a few of us headed there. As this was against the famous Aberdeen, it was always going to be interesting, especially with the fact the Aberdeen Soccer Casuals (ASC) had been coming to Glasgow for a few years and were considered the originals of the early 80s.

This was an era where you could pay to get into the match, and you could choose where you wanted to be. So, we'd get in quite early and take up our seats in the bottom tier of the main stand. A few impressive faces we knew started coming in from the off – numbers were increasing and we were always crowd watching – checking out the latest styles. The threads had moved on from sportswear, cords and footwear. Paisley-patterned shirts and fishing jackets were the new chosen attire a few of the crew were carrying the wee black brolly accessory. Hair was now short!

This was a total buzz being amongst the likeminded lads. Celtic's own brand of this counterculture was up and running, the new style stemming from football. I was wearing said paisley shirt buttoned up to the top, with cords slit at the bottom and desert boots; boys were becoming men. The Celtic fans thought they had got rid of their casuals due to the fact they couldn't locate the ski hats on the terraces anymore. But what was developing opposite them in the main stand was a bigger crew that had evolved.

Some Aberdeen supporters took up seats in the row at the back of us wearing their red and white scarfs. They must have thought they would have the comfort of a nice view from sitting down instead of the terracing. Until the mutton brains saw us. There was a slightly odd feeling to this match as it was days after our legendary manager Jock Stein had lost his life in Cardiff whilst managing Scotland. There was a minute silence before kick-off that was observed impeccably by both sets of supporters, as well as a top gesture was displayed from the Aberdeen fans as they laid out a red and white wreath behind the goals in memory of Big Jock.

During the match, we were looking over at the away end to locate the Aberdeen casuals amongst their support; they had brought a lot of fans down as they always did. The league was usually a race between us and them so they would always fill one half of the old away end. Celtic took the lead in the first half and the stadium erupted. We were all bouncing up and down in the main stand chanting, "Celtic Soccer Crew" hoping to be noticed. A few of our lads couldn't resist flipping back and landing on the laps of the Aberdeen mutton brains in the back row of the bottom section. Some of the Celtic lads were pretending to be stuck as they tried to push us off, "Get aff" in that Aberdeen accent was the cry, while signalling to the police.

After all this had calmed down, we became aware to our right that a load of ASC had come into the no man's land (which was a wee section of terracing that was usually kept clear between the away end and the main stand) but they had moved in to check us out.

To give them credit, they had big numbers but we started chanting at them. They started hand signalling mocking the size of us compared to them. They had a few more older lads but we knew that was always the case in these early days. Aberdeen were smartly turned out wearing a lot of darker colours looking very anti-suss. Just then the police moved into them and pushed the ASC ushering them back to the main part of the away end.

Aberdeen equalised late in the game which was about to become a flat beer moment with this being a top of the table clash and, of course, the smuggy mutton brains in our face chanting, "Aberdeen, Aberdeen, Aberdeen" like a theme tune to the depression!

With minutes to go, as was the Celtic way, Brian McClair scored the winner (2-1). With utter delirium in the ground, we tried to accidentally fall back on the muttons in the back row again but they were running to get out the stand – a poor show as we only wanted a kiss and a hug!

Celtic won the match. It was now game on with the ASC. We left the ground together and tried to turn left past the old Celtic shop, but we noticed a barrier was up to stop this so we headed straight down and gathered at the bus stop opposite the London Road primary school. There were a lot Celtic fans leaving the ground moving both ways on London Road. About five minutes later, we noticed the mounted police moving from the away end towards us. That was when we knew they had the away fans and the ASC with them as they tried to keep them at the other side of the road.

Given the amount of scarfers, it was quite easy to mingle so we went on the move towards Aberdeen. As we became face to face with them, they used their experience from fighting our fans previously and charged at us first, backing us off. Also fans with their kids fled as that was the only option they had.

We gathered again across the street just up from the bus stop and we moved up London Road. A few of our main faces grabbed us and we got switched on. This time we led the charge at Aberdeen. I can recall the mix of apprehension and adrenaline at fifteen years old, having it toe to toe with the ASC. This was Glasgow and it's Celtic at home so we weren't budging. There were a few hundred going for it but it was lucky if we could land more than a couple punches. I can also recall seeing the infamous golf ball with nails in it, flying through the air as well as being cracked with a few

283

black brollies. I remember taking a few dull ones but not feeling anything. This became quite an addiction from this season onwards.

A few of our lot were getting grabbed by the plod and being told it was our last warning. Due to the big numbers back then, we outnumbered the police on a big scale. It was a nightmare for them. The plod managed to contain us and the ASC on either side of London Road as we walked further towards Bridgeton. We were now just posturing and getting a good look at the ASC. You could check out their look: no bright colours, very anti-suss with a lot of obscure Adidas trainers. Out of nowhere, someone in our mob lobbed a bottle of Irn Bru into the middle of the Aberdeen mob and with that, we followed through over to them. They certainly stood their ground and again it kicked off. Nobody got a result as we were all eventually split.

This was my first real taste of it and I was hooked on all of it. Don't ever stop the dance.

Keith M (The Farm) – Everton

It'll be '77–'79 focused on my introduction to what was initially called smoothie/scally, the origins of what would become casual, and the group of lads I hung around and went to the games with. They consisted of both Everton and Liverpool fans, called the classic mob. They were the original Liverpool Road End and Everton Park End lads. We supported different teams yet would go to each other's away games just for the graft and the usual mayhem, but we would have died for each other.

This won't be a story of violence, but of youth, loyalty, that feeling of belonging and togetherness. It was for a short period of time, but it's stayed with me all these years. I still see some of the very same lads now, only now and then, but all of those memories come flooding back. It's like being seventeen again – fresh out of school, unemployed, no chance of work, bonding around football, music and fashion. Although we didn't know it as fashion then, that came later when others would adopt it. I've no idea where it came from, or why it came about. I met it at a school disco in St Bede's Catholic High School in the form of Ged Thomas and Clarky, at the tender age of sixteen. That next week, I'd be off to a mid-week League Cup game against Stockport County.

Colin W – West Ham

Becoming a Hammers Fan

Why do I support West Ham? I was born and brought up close to Upton Park and could walk to the ground easily. I was taken to my first match by a West Ham supporter from the council estate I lived on. It was West Ham versus Sheffield United, 6th November 1971. We lost 2-1, but that did not matter, as standing on the South Bank, I can still picture the floodlights coming on in the second half and hearing the singing. It was very exciting for a youngster.

From 1974-75 onwards, I missed very few home games. Watching players, such as Billy Bonds, Trevor Brooking, Frank Lampard, Keith Robson, Billy Jennings, Tommy Taylor, Kevin Lock, John McDowell, Graham Paddon and Clyde Best, trying to play passing football and actually appearing to want to play for the club. We had the managers Ron Greenwood and John Lyall who emphasised the passing game.

What Is Special About the Club?

The support, in terms of loyalty, humour and some of the characters you encounter. Many memories of great games, like the home tie against Eintracht Frankfurt in the second leg of the semi-final of the European Cup Winners' Cup in 1975. Winning at Wembley in 1980 (especially as we were the underdogs) and the play-off finals in Cardiff and Wembley versus Preston and Blackpool.

I've also been on some memorable away trips on Lacey's coaches, the Irons Travel Club, with the use of Persil train tickets and a student railcard. The Anti-Bond protest with various imaginative demonstrations also sticks in the mind.

The Hammer used to be one of the best match day programmes, pocket sized, with great photographs, match reports and detail. I've based my comments on the club with reference to the fans and the teams as opposed to those who appear to run the club. The administration of the club has always been a mystery to me, in terms of its secrecy. There has been little transparency in the way the club has been run. But I will continue to support West Ham United for a number of reasons. I still enjoy going to the game despite the increased commercialisation of the Premier League, with its growing number of soulless plastic grounds and corporate middle tiers, as I get to meet up with my mates. Many of whom no longer live locally to me.

There is also always, of course, the hope that one day we will be run properly as a football club and achieve some success on the football pitch.

Update 2020

I was delighted to be asked by Jason to contribute to the book. During lockdown, I've had plenty of time to write new West Ham material, but until I was asked, following a trip to Wroxham to visit Bonzo, I was really not bothered about putting pen to paper (or voice dictation to my Mac, as I now have Parkinson's).

Going through an old collection of Newham Recorder newspaper cuttings brought back many memories of great home and away games. The photography of Stevie Bacon is legendary.

The book *There's Only One Stevie Bacon* is well worth a read. He was one of the very few people to be allowed into Upton Park when we beat Real Castilla in 1980, in a behind closed doors European Cup Winners' Cup game, capturing a match with many great shots.

One of the best photographs he ever took was of David Cross celebrating his fourth goal at White Hart Lane; a great night out captured in a black and white still. He also captured the mood of the 1992 pitch protests over the club's bond scheme, with some great photographs including one with the headline: "Lying Thieving Cheats."

The fashion aspect of terrace culture has always fascinated me. Looking smart and wearing decent clothes is an important part of match day. It was noticeable years ago that you could identify supporters by the brands they would wear. For example, I still associate the Rockport brand as historically a very Liverpool item of clothing, with Transalpine now in the ascendency, a clever innovative brand harping back to the musical influences of Joy Division and others.

Watching football has changed enormously since I first went in the 1970s. A combination of ridiculous kick-off times dedicated and dictated by worldwide television money for a game at the other end of the country is indicative of the commercialisation of the game. There is little, if any, consideration for those who travel to matches. Satellite and cable television companies move fixtures around almost at will, ignoring the sheer inconvenience to long-suffering supporters who really want to be at the match. Many supporters no longer go to games either because of expense, inconvenient kick-off times, or feeling marginalised from their clubs, preferring instead the luxury of their armchair, local social club (if still opened) or pub lounge (again, if still open).

Terrace culture has many commentators who have made clear that it has changed beyond recognition. I myself much prefer now going to non-league games, where you watch players actually trying their hardest to win and to perform for the clubs. Local players who know what a local derby means as opposed to those distant millionaire players far removed from everyone's day-to-day experience. The non-league grounds are much quirkier and interesting compared to the sterile sanitised new shopping bowls that masquerade as football grounds.

(I feel this piece from Colin touches on how the game has gone from its working-class roots to being less user friendly with huge ticket prices, massive restrictions, rubbish kick-off times blah blah blah. But I think he's right.)

Keith – Liverpool

An out of towner's viewpoint: there was no being born into a club, local community or following the pack. My elder brother had followed Chelmsford City (Southern League) home and away in the late 60s into the early 70s. His group all decided to adopt a first division club. Some choose London teams. I seem to recall there also being Ipswich, Everton and, in his case (plus a couple of others), Liverpool Football Club. They would still watch Chelmsford, but also would go to see their newly claimed club(s). Football wasn't such a big deal in the family home, so I followed my big brother.

During my school years, most of my matches would be trips to the capital and reasonably nearby grounds. My first trip to Anfield was in April 1977 (aged fourteen) sitting in the Main Stand. I spent a lot of the match looking over at the swaying masses standing on The Kop.

Once I was sixteen and in full time employment, money was my own and travelling further afield was a must. Fortunately, back then, the majority of matches were Saturdays with a 15:00 kick-off. The LFC London Branch normally booked a couple of carriages on a train, departing Euston soon after 08:00. The first cans would be opened before the train even saw daylight outside of the station. The travellers were of varying ages. Many had moved down from the north west seeking work. Others, like myself, had found a connection. It was a great way of meeting people with varied lifestyles, but all had LFC in common. Arriving on a train from London, with a southern accent, meant that at away games you were largely left alone and could go for a beer wherever you fancied before heading to the match. The 80s were fast approaching and the appearance of the younger generation of football supporters was changing. It felt great looking smart.

Travelling to Liverpool gave a different fashion approach and style compared to where I lived. It gave an identity without wearing colours, except for maybe the small pin badge the size of a small fingernail with a Liver bird upon it. There were matches where there could be several different sets of supporters travelling. Normally all went okay, after a few sarky comments of glory hunters etc. had been passed, but it was realised that you were all match going supporters (in short, while all opposing the government, in particular Colin Moynihan and his ID card proposal). Coming back from Carlisle in the Cup, the train had started in Glasgow. By the time we arrived back in London, there were Glasgow Rangers, Carlisle, and Liverpool respective London branch supporters' clubs. Bournemouth had been at Blackpool, Villa at Crewe, and a couple more sets as the train headed south. A great trip was to be had.

Mid-weekers were a killer, getting the last train out of Lime Street and arriving at Euston at about 05:30 the following morning. Then when the service changed, it would involve changing trains at Crewe. The introduction of TV football, not MOTD, but live televised matches and drastic changes to train timetables has for the likes of myself made the M6 a more regular route to matches. It's not quite the same, but at the end of the day, I'm out for a social day. It may not always feel that way when I'm getting off the coach nowadays after a European night, and the realisation of going into work within a couple of hours sinks in. Great days and great times but would love to move back from these sterile times to the 70s and 80s when I became addicted to attending football matches.

Jay from Salford – Man U

My first game at Old Trafford was against Norwich in 1976. I was nine years old and after seeing the heaving masses on the Stretford End, there was definitely something inside my head saying, "I want to be a part of this." My father was a big United fan and Salford is still a stronghold of support for the team. I think there were only three City fans in the whole of our secondary school.

Come the start of the 80s, I was a typical thirteen-year-old. Car washing, golf caddying, I even did a milk round (not the greatest job in winter) to get money for United and clothes. All the lads round our way were obsessed with sportswear and we had some really decent shops in Manchester, Gansgear, Hurley's, Tyldesley and Halbrooks (an old-style cricket and sports store, but they'd have Patrick suedes in and sometimes rare Adidas tennis shoes). Even Top Shop was great for Adidas in those days.

Kendal's was another good store, Sabre jumpers, Lacoste, Pringle for that early 80s look. Luckily, most of us could source from home and not have to travel to other towns and cities. Just down the road from us, we had Strangeways. Back then, you could get Fiorucci, Lois, all the good stuff for a really decent price off the wholesalers. It wasn't the capital of snide that it is now. Plus, there were quite a few hiking shops for the coats (lots of need in the rainy city). There was a heck of a lot of one-upmanship around then. You'd buy something that was "in" and a couple of weeks later, it would be "well out". You'd be heavily criticised, God help you, if you went on holiday with the folks only to return and find everyone had moved on to other things.

United in those days were a decent Cup team with a great following. Nothing more, nothing less. Really, it was more fun on the terraces than watching some of the games. After the highs of watching Tommy Docherty's attacking football, it was a bit of a comedown under Dave Sexton. I soon started getting to away games. First on the match specials, then the Persils (reckon my mum had about two years' worth of soap powder under her sink at one stage) and the buzz increased. I loved going away with United. It was always eventful, especially at Merseyside. We'd have some right battles with them.

You sort of passed your apprenticeship if you went to Everton or Liverpool away in those days.

Around spring '83, I noticed a lot of lads at the match stopped wearing the ridiculously expensive stuff and adopted (well, to me it was) a classic look of cagoule/ smock/fisherman's coat, button down collar check shirt, M&S crewneck, parallel or slightly flared cords or jeans and trainers, like Adidas Indoor Supers or the rare City Series (that you could only get in a market store called Oasis). We'd go to places like QPR and be laughed at by the locals, while we'd be laughing at their lads for looking the same as every other London team. If we went up to the north east, you'd have beer monsters screaming abuse like we were aliens. I loved all that. We all had a "Manchester, we do things differently here" attitude towards most things, definitely in relation to what we wore.

I was going to the odd nightclub (Rotters, Pips, Placemate 7 and a cracking reggae club called The PSV) but was more interested in going to see bands. I liked a lot of indie stuff and there were shows on in town most nights. I will always remember the day (in '85) a cracking lad from round our way (Bob Spencer RIP) mentioned his mate was a drummer in a band and told me about a gig they were doing, "You like your indie, Jay, don't yer?

There's some lads I know playing Corbiere's next week. They're called The Happy Mondays. They're all Salford reds. You'll love 'em." It was their fourth ever gig.

Before they played a note, I knew I was going to like them as Gaz and Paul were both wearing Gazelles. Half the crowd (they were the support band) were some of Salford's finest degenerates and characters. All you could smell was weed and the other half of the audience were looking at us all in dread thinking their coats and bags were going to be stolen.

A lot of United and City lads were soon following the band. It was always a good night. One gig at The International had loads of people hiding under tables on bad acid. Me and my mate were wondering what the f**k was going on, but Shaun on stage knew (probably someone in the group supplied them) and started heckling them, trying to freak them all out for a laugh. There was never a normal show, just complete madness. I was getting on the guest list every gig because my brother knew their manager. I absolutely loved those times. I always thought of them as "our" band; they weren't a bunch of students in leather trousers talking about their "art" and moaning that their trust fund was running out. I still love 'em to this day. They were supposed to be playing Amsterdam in March (2020) but had to cancel. Me and the better half still went over and spotted loads of Salford and Manchester heads mooching around. It would have been a top night though I reckon the Dutch police breathed a sigh of relief.

Come 1990, I'd managed to steal a job at British Rail, which meant I got free travel, including Europe. I spent the next seven years jibbing around Europe, visiting many of their local sports shops wherever we were playing and we never seemed to spend much at the till. They were absolutely great times. Three-day journeys to Gothenburg, Kosice, Barcelona, Munich during the beer festival, Milan, Budapest and then four or five days to get back (if the police had anything to do with it). There were loads of us on the trains as some enterprising lads we knew had "acquired" interrails for £50 and snide returns from Manchester to Dover for a fiver. You would be sitting on an Ostend-Vienna train for twelve hours, but one of your party would have loads of whiz (his brother made it on a farm in Cheshire). Someone else had a big block of Sputnik, pills would be readily available. Plus two or three crates of beer would always mysteriously arrive just before the train set off, delivered by young lads who seriously didn't give a monkey's and would have walked out of any shop with half their stock if they could carry it.

Another of the young'uns worked at a print shop so we usually had good quality snides to get in. Most of us seemed to have more money coming back than when we set off. I did eleven years of that, maybe six or seven times a season, with obviously the highlight being the 1999 treble.

In 2002, I was attacked by someone with a hammer, got a big fracture of my skull (and it ruined my international modelling career forever...) and basically stopped going to the games. I didn't like the way it was going anyway. I started going to non-league games after the Glazers took over United. It was good for a while, quite a few reds started going and we'd all have a good drink and days out in in mad places like Bacup, Whitby, even Leipzig for a friendly.

I stopped going to that a few years back and just sell my mate's United magazine outside the ground now (or I did 'till bloody COVID-19) and still see a lot of lads from the 80s. There's sadly been a few that have passed away these last few years, including one of the interrail lads (who was only forty-three). Whenever we meet up, there's always conversations about how good the 80s were. I genuinely think I was very lucky to have lived in that era. The football was better, the music definitely was. Madchester, the raves in the late 80s. Sourcing decent clothes was a challenge we were all up for, and luckily there was no CCTV in sports shops/jewellers/train stations! Lads nowadays have got it a lot worse. £40-50 for a match ticket, £90 for a return train ticket to London, then no smoking and £6 a pint in the ground? Then if it does kick off, a few slaps given, up to six-year bans and even jail time? Actually, I feel sorry for them, they'll never know what it was like. Good people who support each other still today.

Jim L – Oxford

Welcome to 1983. The Conservative party are cruising to a landslide victory securing Margaret Thatcher her second term of office, as anti-nuclear demonstrations are on the march throughout Europe, drawing unprecedented numbers not seen since the 60s. An IRA bomb kills six at Harrods in London and CDs, dismissed by purists as a fad, have become generally available on the high street, though it is still unusual to find more than two varieties of lettuce and one of tomato on supermarket shelves. Two years before Live Aid, Duran Duran, The Human League and Spandau Ballet are fighting it out in the charts while elder statesman Bowie is back, putting on his red shoes and dancing the blues.

Me? I'm putting on black Doc Martens, brogues, Levi's, a Donkey jacket and check shirt and waiting for a bus to the football to watch Oxford United. A commotion, shouting, feet on the march, a swaggering swarm getting nearer and nearer. Some breaking into a jog, other groups noisily commandeering taxis. Foreign exchange students, I guess. But as they get closer, I can see they're *sans* rucksack and they're all young males, younger than me even (a fresh-faced twenty-year-old). They certainly look foreign, alien even. What in God's name are they wearing? Then I hear the accent. That's not Boulogne cutting through the early evening air, that's Bermondsey. This is Millwall, our opponents for the evening. It becomes clear that the main group are planning to catch the same bus as me, so it's all aboard and standing room only.

I now get a chance to have a proper look at my fellow travellers' clothes. You have to believe me here, I've seen it all, (and worn most of it). Punk PVC and safety pins, mod revival and the frilly shirts of the much-maligned New Romantics. But this is all new to me. This mob are dressed like a bunch of golfers! That's right, I said golfers. And middle-aged ones at that.

From the waist up, they're wearing an assortment of plain or argyle check jumpers and cardigans, some with polo shirts and many with, forgive me if I'm dreaming this, lightweight roll neck sweaters. Everything seems to be in a pastel shade, blue, lemon yellow, even the odd bit of pink. Logos are everywhere. Pringle lions fighting to get themselves noticed on mazes of diamonds, Lyle & Scott eagles perch on chests and strangest of all, Lacoste crocodiles scuttle round those pristine white roll necks.

Down below, it's all faded or bleached jeans, or brightly coloured corduroys (some have three-inch splits in the outer hem). The footwear of choice seems to be suede desert boots or trainers in dyed suede or white leather. Soon after this, I learnt that the group I had seen were known as "football casuals". Every club in the country had them or soon would and I thought they were the coolest thing I'd ever seen.

It wasn't long before I became one of their number, and for my twenty-first birthday, I received a blue Pierre Cardin jumper and I bought myself a pair of Patrick trainers and a Benetton polo shirt. It took me a while to get it right but by '85, I was swanning around in Paul Smith, Marco Polo and Retour and have dressed as a casual on and off to this day. I still haven't worn a roll neck sweater or put on a pair of red shoes though. That reminds me, how do you dance the blues?

Bob the Mod – West Ham

West Ham and Fashion

It all started for me through football. One of my earliest memories was being in the North Bank watching the silver-booted skins running up the aisle. I was probably nine or ten as I thought they looked like cybermen. Then a couple of years later, our first away game was by bus to Arsenal as two twins had come to our school, Jason and Clifford Fallon. They were Arsenal and round our way that was very unusual. We would have been only eleven or twelve, but we had to get two buses up there and I think we went in the North Bank with the twins and their mates. We got chased by a massive mob of skins after the game. I don't know if they were West Ham or Arsenal but when they came round the corner, we ran and ran.

Around that time, we started going with our neighbour's daughter, Sherilyn, who loved football and usually took four or five of us along. Then we started going on our own with other school mates, meeting outside the station and walking to the ground, saving our bus fare for hot dogs or peanuts. I always had an interest in fashion as did most of our little group: me, my best mate Robert Stubbs, Paul Cumberbatch and Freddy Donaldson. We were probably "soul boys". We were about twelve or thirteen, wearing the latest in pegs and points, but a little bit before who could have the most buttoned high waisters.

Luckily, my nan worked in the rag trade so could knock up whatever was fashionable quickly. Grandad shirts, and check suits were the big thing too around the time, circa 1975-76. Then punk happened. One of our big nights out was the social in the main hall at Forest Gate Maternity Hospital, which we got into because Stubbs' mum worked there. Once, we got in early to play "God Save the Queen". By this time, the trend was a Donkey jacket and DMs during the day, and dressing up at night.

The South Bank was full of boneheads. I don't recall seeing any punks but considering that most people who went to punk gigs wore a Donkey jacket and jeans, no surprises there. Oh, and Paul Neal had bondage trousers but was a skin and never did the straps up so he could run properly. I got the buzz then and was looking for an identity. I really didn't fancy the boneheads as they were all National Front and a lot of my mates were black. Also, a couple of older lads took me to the Bladebone (a notorious NF pub) at the bottom of Brick Lane and one of the noncey leaders kept buying me drinks. It all seemed very odd to me. I didn't like it one bit.

Paul Neal and Glen Pearman knew some of the older lads over there, and they were dressed differently, wearing parkas in the summer of '78. Paul told me they were mods and I thought I'd have some of that. We went up to Mintz and Davies in Romford and I brought a parka and two pairs of Sta Prest (one pair in light blue, the other beige). I already had a couple of Ben Shermans and a Fred Perry. I'd had a crop for about a year. So, there I was, a mod. I painted the back of my parka with The Jam in black and white as part of my art project at school, and got an A. A couple of weeks later, I took Stubbsy up there and parkas were now a tenner. Double what I'd paid a couple of weeks earlier. I bought a pair of tonic trousers this time.

By the following summer of 1979, most of my mates had moved on and "casual" was the new thing with Gabbicis and Farahs replacing parkas and button downs, but for a while the desert boots stayed. I stuck with it, all throughout two-tone. At one point, I was known as "Bob the mod" over West Ham as I was the only one left. I did stick with it for years, running clubs and putting on gigs. The style and certainly the music has stuck with me throughout. No West Ham, no mods!

I must say I watched the casual thing closely as most of my mates were well into it. It mirrored mod so much, listening to imported American soul and reggae, the Italian fashions and the fashions moving so quickly. And the violence. I was coming home from work once and I bumped into my mate's brother Stuart, and he was wearing a blue Sergio but it was covered in plaster. I said, "Stu, why you wearing that to work? They're seventy quid, aren't they?" He said, "Well, all the northerners are wearing them now!" And that is just about one of the most mod things I've ever heard.

Jason I – Middlesborough

I first started going to the footy in the mid-70s, at my beloved Boro and Ayresome Park, with my dad. He had a tendency to always stand me next to the away supporters, hence witnessing the fist fights breaking out, flares and skinheads.

A few years on, and football specials were all the rage. Ska, mods and the early casual scene was kicking in. I f***ing loved it. Going to Leeds, Sheffield, Sunderland, Hull en masse. Going into their pubs, heading for the jukebox, seeing who's wearing what. I'm still obsessed with The Jam, mod, ska and a bit of the jazz funk scene.

In the mid-80s, I worked away. There was no work in the Boro. Thatcher, miners' strikes, docks closing, steelworks etc. So, I got working in Bristol, and travelling up and down on the trains, meeting up with the Boro lads. No colours ever, but tiny club badges were the trend, along with chinos, Lois, Pepe jeans and

310

dungarees (not me). I was still in the footie scene during the really violent era of the mid to late 80s.

Whilst down south, I'd go to see Bristol City, Rovers, Cardiff and many others. Always in the away ends waiting for some action. Eastville still had skins. British bulldog had been sold not far from the notorious St Paul's area. It had a similar feel to the old Den, but with that Wurzel accent I just couldn't get.

In the late 80s, I moved back to the north east. Boro were on a roll with Rioch at the helm. I seem to remember The House Martins, acid house and the early Manc scene. I loved The Stone Roses; they've always been popular with the Boro lads. I'm still staying loyal to Adidas and Harrington. My hair's a bit longer and the wedge style is long gone. Jeans are a little baggy for me.

As the years went on through the 90s and into the millennium, modern football fans emerged with music blasting after a goal, trying to kill the most loyal lads of football. Like it or not, many lads, now older men, are still the most loyal fans clubs have. Those who still turn up when your clubs are sh**e. It's the old casual scene lads you'll see in the pub before and after, all bitter and twisted. But put on some Jam, Beat, Sham 69 etc. and all is forgiven for an hour or so.

Up the Boro.

311

Sean B – Wolves

I was born into a middle-class family with a family business and always lived in the Wolverhampton area. My dad used to take me to the Molineux to watch Wolves in the 70s, where fighting was a regular thing amongst visiting fans and the skins, gangs of town centre drinking men who all had broken noses and laboured on building sites.

I went through the two-tone era of 1979-80, sneaking into the skin and mod clubs as a thirteen-year-old, witnessing a lot of violence between us and local rockers or biker gangs. But the era was defining for us, along with the recession and the Thatcher years. This changed one day when, on a bus, I noticed a lad with a blonde wedge haircut, Adidas Sambas, burgundy cords, a skiing jumper and a green flying jacket, which I found fascinating after years of Doc Martens and Crombie's. I invested in a very similar outfit and, now attending the matches with my mates, I was seeing the fashion evolve from Slazenger, flying jackets and Samba to Pringle, Hunter Leathers, Borg Elite and so on. At the same time, Wolves were being followed by a casual firm known as the Subway Army who led the way in the fashion stakes in Wolverhampton and definitely left their mark on rivals. I was not in the Subway, a little too young and probably from the wrong side of town, but I witnessed them in action several times.

The Subway disbanded late in 1983 after a fatal stabbing during a gang fight in town, and for the 1984-5 season, Wolves had several smaller, unorganised gangs attending, but no solid firm. In '86, I began to attend games regularly again and this time we were getting decent numbers of lads. Those who were on the fringes of the Subway were doing the organising. Wolves were now in the old fourth division and taking 3000 fans away most weeks, mainly lads and p**sheads intent on causing mayhem.

All went well, with us making the news following trouble at Scarborough, Exeter, Bradford and home games against Cardiff, Bolton and Northampton to name a few. Then in February '88, came the 6 a.m. knock, which left my mum in particular, in shock. Twelve hours later, around twenty of us were on the landing in Winson Green, followed later that year by prison sentences handed to dozens of us, in what was and still is, the biggest dawn raid on football violence in the UK. I pulled myself fifteen months and a five-year ban.

The ban was no inconvenience as from 1989-91 most of us were heavily involved with the rave culture, which resulted in shady people, prison sentences, drive-bys, and hugging lads who normally we would be fighting.

The first game back after the ban (in 1993), we had a reunion of all the lads from Operation Growth, at an away game at Port Vale which was eventful; and a massive go with Stoke on the way home on the station platform. Made even better due to the fact we had Stoke away the following week which, as usual up there, was carnage.

I have little to do with football now. I swore not to take my son to Wolves and he played rugby as a young lad, and has now gone on to play professionally and attended university on a rugby scholarship. However, I am very close to the lads from football. I still have a curry with a couple in particular and attend stag dos, weddings, christenings etc. That bond can't be explained to an outsider. You walk in a pub, haven't seen them for years, but the handshake tells it all. You were there, you had my back, just call me if you need help... Glad to have been involved.

Marcus S – Northampton/Newcastle

I can honestly say that I've never gone to the football mob-handed, looking for it, but ended up involved in plenty of scraps. I wasn't of age to get involved until '87. I had always been a football fan, but fashion was important too, and fighting was just normal. I had a split upbringing between family in Newcastle and Northampton, and used to go watch both. I'd even watch non-league or schoolboy footie for something to do. These were days when we had four television channels, pre-Sky, no internet or mobiles. Mid-week internationals were on the radio.

Dressing the part came naturally. The stuff in the boutiques then were amazing. Giorgio Armani had just started his jeans label. Valentino, Ciao, Best Company, Ball jeans, all top-class Italian brands. Chipie, Chevignon, Verte Vallee from France. They had one thing in common though: a week's wages for a single piece. If you went to football with a bit of clobber on, you were assumed to be involved. Home lads would give you the nod, the crack. Opposition fans would give you plenty more than that just for having the look.

I ended up moving full time to Northampton. There were better work prospects and a handier pitch for going to sport. Mainly Northampton, but if Newcastle were in the Midlands or London, I'd go. If only to catch up with my mates. Chalk and cheese.

Northampton had about a hundred regular away fans and on average about twenty were casuals. They really stuck out in small towns, came on top a lot as the police wanted us to get a hiding. One of the worst I got was in Walsall. We'd changed trains at Brum and went on the piss and got split up having a carry on with some Scousers in the dungeons that are New Street station. I missed the train, got the next one and stupidly got off at Walsall instead of Bescot. I had a wander around trying to get my bearings and a clue where the ground was. I thought, *F**k it, get a McDonalds and a taxi to the ground, it can't be far.*

I stood in the queue and, without even opening my mouth, five lads stormed in to give me a crack and a proper stamping. I know why. I was wearing dungarees, a flowery shirt and Kickers, and those monkeys in Walsall were six months behind the trends. I was the sore thumb. If I'd had a chance to speak, I'd be fine, just use my Geordie accent and bulls**t that I was visiting a student mate. I'd pulled that one in a few pubs, always successfully.

Once in Telford (Shrewsbury), I ended up asking if anyone fancied going to the game and getting stuck into some Northampton, and ended up having to listen, straight-faced, how they'd smashed us up at our place. Newcastle was different, as soon as you got anywhere for a train change, there would be hundreds of Geordies travelling from everywhere and they would just take over towns. Pubs were crammed with Newcastle and it was volatile, but in fairness the scarfers were just as much nutters as the main firm.

I was clubbing a fair bit then. Acid house was just getting going and this is my vivid memory of a change. Leicester away, November '89. On the piss near the ground, into the away end, caged in. At halftime, I moved about to see if I could find anyone I knew. A bunch of lads dancing about were the best dressed I'd seen: Paraboot, not Timberlands. Armani eagle knits, not Chipie, smoking spliffs and gave me a go. So, we're having a chat and I ended up scoring a couple of trips off them.

It didn't happen overnight and building up to Italia '90 was naughty, but where a few alliances were formed. By then, I was bumping into more lads from different places I knew through the warehouse scene and Ibiza, and the edge dropped. At Blackburn, I once thought, *Right, it's going off properly.* I got off the train and was it f**k? No. It was just a few of their lads wanting to knock some pills out and tell us where the illegal do was that night.

I've been an expat in Asia for twenty years now and most of my mates have similar backgrounds through football and the club scene. Good chances are we've had a go at or raved with each other in the long and distant (not well-remembered) past, but one thing is for sure, we all think, *What the f**k were we doing?* Rowing, getting nicked, what a load of bol***ks but great fun, adrenaline, excitement. At the time, that's where ecstasy played its role and took over.

Vaughny – TBF

I was about in the early 70s. My first away game was Liverpool, November 1974. We drew 1-1. I was sixteen years old. I was taught by older people, Big Ted and Bill Gardner. They taught me about life and backing people up, and loyalty to each other. We were more like a family. Very few went to away games. In those days, it was the same people at every one. We had morals, something people today don't have anymore. People in the 70s were completely different from the 80s firms of casuals, and people wearing £100 jumpers and jackets.

When we came into the 80s, we were like dinosaurs. We never moved with the times. Our firm really didn't have a name. We just called it Bill and Ted's firm, an offshoot of the Teddy Bunter firm started in the late 60s. In the end, football was a drug to us. We never missed a game, went everywhere: Europe, Communist Russia and Romania. While the Old Bill was so busy pushing about people in good clothes, we were having a field day. We wandered about, causing mayhem. I had an Ellesse tracksuit top. My mate Terry S nicked loads in Germany and gave some to me, still with the price tag on, equivalent to £55, and that was in 1983.

Two years ago, my missus, who is from Thailand, said she was throwing a load of clothes out. I looked and saw this jacket, still virtually brand new. I still wear it now. Those sorts of clothes never bothered us. In the 70s, we were wearing Donkey jackets and DMs, Levi jackets and jeans. I've been at games where only thirty of us were there in the 70s. The best mates I ever had came from football, and we're still mates today. Football was a drug, like someone jacking up. It was the best time of my life.

After it all finished for me, it was about 1990. I have been living in Thailand for thirty years now.

(Vaughny represents one of the most respected factions ever to come out of West Ham. It's good to see another spin from the casual movement. I think the TBF were more about pride for their manor and the team and culture surrounding the club and area. Not all were from the East End but those who were on board signed up in a big way. This book, and us trying to put our case across, *Understanding Terrace Culture* signs into this concept. You didn't have to come from that particular area. It took a lot of guts to do this and some took a lot of stick, but some of the most staunch guys I ever met were from other manors.)

H – Wolverhampton Wanderers

When Jason asked me to put a few words together on terrace culture for his book, I was scratching my head as to where to start. You see, I was never a top lad or a terrace legend and I very much consider myself to be a normal bloke. I have made some great friends from football and have visited getting on sixty football grounds whilst watching my team. So, let's start at the beginning.

Born in Wolverhampton in 1971, there was only ever going to be one club for me. I have early childhood memories of going to home games, rocking up to Molineux minutes before kick off with my old man in his green Hillman Hunter and watching the game from the Waterloo Road enclosure alongside the pitch. I remember one game in particular. Wolves were playing Leeds and there was a real buzz around Molineux. The atmosphere was electric and at halftime, a small group of Wolves fans ran across the pitch into the travelling

Leeds contingent, throwing kicks and punches in what could only be described as a suicide mission. I was fascinated by the crowd around us. Teenage lads engaging in banter decked out in Benetton rugby shirts, Pringle jumpers, Lacoste polo shirts and classic Adidas trainers. I loved it. They dressed so sharp and despite only being around eight or nine years old, I wanted to be a part of it.

At the age of eleven, my family moved to Maidenhead in Berkshire. My extremely broad Black Country accent stood out like a sore thumb and attracted a lot of attention. Some of it good-natured mickey taking but others used it as a way of tormenting me. My accent faded, but one group in particular continued their taunts for a couple of years by mimicking how my father spoke. This saw me get into scraps and confrontations a-plenty. Never the hardest, I always retaliated. Each battle made me all the more proud of my Black Country heritage and cemented my love for Wolverhampton Wanderers.

Three years later, I returned to Wolverhampton and I found myself going to Molineux, with friends from school, as often as possible. Whilst I was in exile, Wolves had fallen from the top flight into the old fourth division. As I turned seventeen, Steve Bull rocked up to

Molineux to sign for Wolves in his Ford Cortina and so my Wolves adventures really began. Our fall from grace allowed us to visit lots of new grounds as we started to climb the leagues, watching Bully bang the goals in.

The Bridge Boys were in full effect before West Midlands police arrested a large number of Wolves fans in Operation Growth (Get Rid of Wolverhampton's Troublesome Hooligans). Both before and after the raids, Wolves would travel around the country, quite often with over seven hundred lads, from different parts of the town and surrounding areas. There were groups from Telford, Gornal, Stourbridge, Cannock, Willenhall, Wednesfield, Darlaston, Fordhouses and Codsall to name a few. These lads all came together on match day. We all have tales a-plenty from away games in places such as Southend, Blackpool, Torquay, Swindon, Middlesbrough, Huddersfield, Leicester, Bradford, Wrexham, Cardiff, Stoke, Port Vale, Tranmere... the list goes on.

We drank in our village during the week, venturing into town for a night out at the weekend. Often travelling to away games in our own group. We didn't really mix with the lads who made up the main Wolves crew, although we knew and respected each other. A lad turned up to a game in a camouflage jacket with a black badge on the arm. It was like a work of art, a real game changer. Within weeks, we were all clamouring for Stone Island, travelling to Newcastle Under Lyme, Manchester and Nottingham to buy the best pieces. Over the years, we wore the lot: Henri Lloyd, CP Company, Boneville, Ma Strum, Lacoste, Burberry, Aquascutums, Ralph Lauren, Soviet, Sergio Tacchini, Ellesse, Fila, Rockport, Timberland, Adidas and so on.

Music was never far away, with our escapades backed by a soundtrack made up of The Jam, The Specials, Oasis, Blur, The Stone Roses, New Order and The Happy Mondays, before moving into the rave scene which took hold, changing the whole direction of the casual movement, but I guess that's another story.

More recently, I have travelled to Europe to watch Nuno Espirito Santo's incredible side in the Europa League. We have come a long way since Steve Bull's Ford Cortina pulled onto the Molineux car park. I am travelling with the same lads who were at the games with me over thirty years ago. For me, terrace culture is a mix of football, clothing and music. But most of all, it's about my mates.

Dave C – QPR

I am now fifty-three years old and, to be honest, I do not go to many games. I now live in Donegal in Ireland, and add to that the COVID situation, it is not easy to travel over. This is not a sob story, but let's say I had a difficult childhood. Mum had her troubles and split with my dad when I was young. There was a lot of drunkenness and violence in my home with her new boyfriend. Mum's fella took me to my first QPR game in the 1977/78 season. I remember it was against Wolves and we stood in the school end, meant for away fans. A lot of QPR fans still went in there as the entry fee was cheaper than the home sections. We lost 3-1. I remember a huge black fella called Bob Hazell played in the Wolves' defence. He later came to play for the R's.

I became best mates with Martin at school. We both started to go to the games together and whatever money we could get hold of went on football and buying vinyl records. At Shepherd's Bush, there was a record exchange down the Goldhawk Road. We were both into punk and I also got right into Oi! skinhead music. Our ritual was to go to the record shop, then have a sausage sarnie in the café by the Underground station. We would then manage to get a bottle of cider each, even though we were only fourteen years old.

The first aggro I ever saw at QPR was against Cardiff, around 1980. It was kicking off, all down the South Africa Road and we saw a taff get a brick over his head. This was so exciting. I had already started fighting at school, and football now became an ideal place to vent out all my anger and troubles from home.

In 1981, the casual scene started to take right off. Me and Martin had saved up some money to go on the train to Leeds away. We won 1-0 and everyone was in high spirits on the way home. I was still a skinhead and Martin was a punk. I wore a scruffy old sheepskin coat. The older lads had a firm called the C-Mob, and I looked up to them and wanted to be like them. It was like a sense of belonging to a tight knit QPR family. One of the lads told me to smarten up and said we were good lads. I took it on board and decided to be a casual myself.

When we got back to London, there was a good off with Gooners outside King's Cross. In those days, there would be loads of different firms milling around the stations looking for it. It would be like a game of "guess the mob". Sometimes after a home game, a load of us would head up to St Pancras, Euston or King's Cross for some fun.

The first bit of clobber I managed to scrape the money together for, was a Patrick wind-cheater. I felt the nuts and the following seasons were my favourite ever times at QPR. From the early 80s onwards, QPR had a decent firm and we were well-dressed too. The famous clothing shop Stuarts was on our doorstep, and lads from all over the country would travel to get their latest gear from there.

QPR won the old Division 2 and went up to the top flight. We started playing the big boys like Man United, Liverpool, Spurs, Arsenal and the like. We would hold our own in the rows with the big boys and sometimes even gave teams like Spurs and Man United a shock. I used to love the away games and there was a little group of about ten of us that went to as many games as we could. We would end up with a bigger mob and have some great times. Leeds away is a stand-out game for me personally, for the sheer adrenaline of the day. I went up with the C-Mob on a coach. We went in the seats above the away terrace, even though we lost 2-1 and got knocked out of the FA Cup, the Leeds fans still wanted to kill us! We literally had to hold it like Custer's last stand and when I say it was hairy it's an understatement.

My love for QPR has cost me more than money. I've been in prison twice and have served four banning orders. If I am to be honest, my problems with alcohol impacted on me being a loose cannon, hence why I kept getting nicked when the other lads knew when to reign it in if the Old Bill turned up. I got sober fifteen years ago and I've not been in trouble since. I still love meeting the lads and every season, we have a big away day out. Last season, we played Luton, our old enemy, for the first time in years. The turnout of old faces that day was superb, and all the old stories were shared.

That old saying, "QPR 'till I die" sure applies to me. I wrote a book about my troubles and a lot about football is in there too. It is on Amazon, called *Beating My Demons*.

Bob N – West Ham

Born March 1962 in Essex.

My dad was a German POW and he passed away in 1968.

Went to a boarding school in Slough in 1970. All the boys supported different teams: Chelsea, Arsenal, West Ham, Spurs, QPR, Palace... They were London kids and northern kids. Liverpool, Man United, Leeds. At the weekend, we would jump on a train to London and see any game. We just loved football.

My best mate was Michael Gunner from Chalk Farm who was Arsenal. What a surname. But coming from Essex, I said West Ham was my team and that's how it started. My sister was into football and we went together. Mum also came sometimes or I would go with my neighbour and his son. Didn't go every week but by 1975, I was going to most home games and local away.

Highlight was the FA Cup run. I remember going in the North Bank, Highbury with Mum, sister and

Michael. He wasn't happy at the end of the game but what a great early birthday present for me.

Also went to Villa Park for the semi-final versus Ipswich with neighbour and son.

Sunday morning went to Upton Park for replay tickets, but all sold out. Mum bought three tickets off a tout for £5 each.

On Cup final day, Mum, my sister and I got an early train from Chelmsford. We went straight to Wembley Park station. First tout Mum saw, she got three tickets which were £12 each. They happened to be Fulham End, but we were in.

By the 1977 season, I started getting the train from Chelmsford with school mates and other local lads who I am still mates with today.

Like most kids our age, we started in the North Bank with scarves around our wrists and necks, wearing jean jackets with patches on.

Then it was the good old Donkey jacket, DMs or Monkey boots followed by green Flight jackets, Fred Perry, Ben Sherman, desert boots then Pringle, Lyle & Scott jumpers, Farah and Kickers boots.

Transport to games up north was football specials, minibuses, Transit Luton vans, intercity coaches or cars.

Early days, home games.

I would get the train from Chelmsford to Stratford sometimes. I would just get a platform ticket or return to Shenfield and bunked through the barrier at Stratford.

First stop would be pie and mash then get to Boleyn for opening time. In there was hardcore fans who over the years have become top mates.

Alan Bax – Port Vale

As a young boy in the early to mid-70s, my father took me to watch matches at his beloved Stoke City. I witnessed street battles with many big clubs. Sometimes very scary as we walked back to the car. In 1978, when I was thirteen, we went to an Easter match at Blackpool. Stoke's massive firm ran riot, before, during and after.

At fourteen, I became a programme seller at little Port Vale for extra pocket money. At Christmas, my family begrudgingly bought me a "rival" Vale scarf. On New Year's Day, I was selling programmes in the snow, when a group of three Huddersfield yobs stole my scarf. Some handy-looking Vale supporters arrived and asked why I was upset. They retrieved my scarf and gave the trio a gentle slapping. I thanked them, before one of the Vale crew said, "No problem. Any friend of Vale is a friend of mine." All of a sudden, I felt part of something special, like a bond, and from then on, I was hooked.

1979 on Easter Friday. Stoke had no home match (I sold programmes there too) so I went with a Port Vale fan to see them at Springfield Park, Wigan Athletic. I was surprised by the size of the Port Vale mob, and how game they were. A mixture of skinheads, punks and casually dressed supporters of all ages fought running battles in a ground with no segregation. This time I felt excitement, mixed with fear, as I looked for protection from more experienced terraced warriors, who didn't disappoint.

By 1981, I was seventeen and had matured in confidence, enjoying terrace banter and being part of the paddock mob. Not a ringleader, but I used to thrive on the thrills of match day rivalry, and striving to help build our reputation amongst the hooligan culture in the lower leagues. I loved the clothes too. My favourites being my iced blue jeans and yellow Pringle jumper. Occasionally I would wear tie-dyed bleached jeans and a sheepskin. There are songs that take me back to those magical days. Usually ones that had been played at halftime remind me of particular matches, such as:

- 1978 Blackpool 1-1 Stoke – "Pictures of Matchstick Men" by Status Quo
- 1979 Rochdale 0-2 Vale – "Three Minute Hero" by The Selector

- 1980 Doncaster 2-0 Vale – "The Tide is High" by Blondie
- 1981 Lincoln 2-2 Vale – "Under Pressure" by Queen and David Bowie
- Between 1982-84, songs by Human League, Heaven 17, ABC, Depeche Mode, Style Council etc. all complemented our football fashions of the time.

I have fond memories from away day summer weekends in Blackpool and Torquay, where I would trade my Pringle and jeans for Union Jack shorts and my Billy Idol bleached hair. In 1983, I hitchhiked to Luxembourg to watch England, draped in my PVFC Union Jack... In my mind, I was representing my club internationally. I have never seen so much carnage as at this game. It was too much, and I felt for the locals. I like to think of myself as a decent person with good ethics and morals. I see things differently nowadays, and just want to go to the game safely and in peace with others. Nothing, however, can take away the excitement of match day confrontations with rivals at home, and on away days. Am I right in saying that we weren't necessarily bad or nasty people, just caught up in this infectious culture that was around at the time?

Every club, even the smallest ones like Halifax, Torquay and Rochdale, would have mobs protecting their patch. In 1987, I was arrested at Tranmere for threatening behaviour. This put my RAF career on the line, and so from that day, I backed off somewhat.

Full Time...

It's entering the final few minutes of the game. Part of me is happy to take a well-deserved point. After all, we got away with it for so many years and thankfully no one got really hurt (not on my watch anyway) and a few laughs were had and a few lessons were learnt. Rivalries were a-plenty and respect was abundant. The look and the walk was the order of the day. Friendships were made and adventures were had. The era gave me something to be part of in a time of change which left some of us old school Herbert's a bit dazed and confused!

I'd like to say that we might nick the win in the dying seconds of the game but in that way of life, there weren't really any winners, just surviving and having the crack was enough. After all, who really wants to boast about being the best around when for me just being part of something a bit left field and maybe a bit beyond the pale and a bit renegade was enough. There really wasn't ever going to be a career or fame and in the end, it would have caught up with us and some it did!

Through some good advice, mainly from John D, Sid B, Dad, Old Man Patsy, Lynn and Kev, George B and Karen, Adam S, Dad, Bill and a few other good men and women, I hung up my boots and retired gracefully.

I met a girl who would change my life (thank you, Lee and Lisa) and one who I want to spend the rest with. I love my kids and my two dogs Bert and Claude, and am doing okay!

Would I do it again? Would I be part of something like the football casuals' scene again? Well, that's a good question. Having lived through it already and having scraped through, the younger angry adventurous side of me might say yes. But the older wiser side would say no! I had many great laughs, many adventures and a few regrets, but deep down would probably pass on doing it all again based just on the fact that we did get the draw and didn't push our luck and we are here to tell the tale!

Living through the horrible year of 2020 and not knowing what's around the corner, it gave me time to gather my thoughts and try to do something positive and get through by being creative. It also gave the contributors some inspiration too and have been thanked by many for letting them share their experiences and maybe vent a little! Hope you enjoyed.

P.S. I had a soft spot for Wham really!

Printed in Great Britain
by Amazon